Fostering Information Literacy

Information Literacy Series

Fostering Information Literacy

Connecting National Standards, Goals 2000, and the SCANS Report

Helen M. Thompson

Susan A. Henley

Foreword by Daniel D. Barron

2000
Libraries Unlimited, Inc.
and Its Division
Teacher Ideas Press
Englewood, Colorado

Libraries Unlimited, Inc.
and Its Division
Teacher Ideas Press
P.O. Box 6633
Englewood, CO 80155-6633
1-800-237-6124
www.lu.com
www.lu.com/tip

Library of Congress Cataloging-in-Publication Data

Thompson, Helen M.
    Fostering information literacy : connecting national standards, Goals 2000, and the SCANS report / Helen M. Thompson, Susan A. Henley.
        p. cm. -- (Information literacy series)
    Includes bibliographical references and index.
    ISBN 1-56308-767-7
    1. Information retrieval--Study and teaching (Elementary)--United States. 2. United States. Goals 2000: Educate America Act. 3. United States. Dept. of Labor. Secretary's Commission on Achieving Necessary Skills I. Title. II. Series. III. Henley, Susan A.

ZA3075.T47   1999
025.5'24'071 21--dc21   99-041692
                                                                                    CIP

In memory of my mother, Pauline Ayers.

—SAH

In honor of my family, especially my husband, Scott.

—HMT

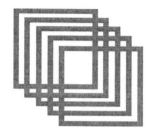

Contents

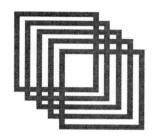

List of Figures and Tables

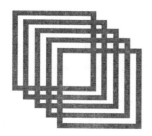

Foreword

The authors of *Crystal Fire: The Birth of the Information Age* set the stage well for the book you are about to read and use: "In this age power accrues to those who can ride and guide the torrent of information available."[1] Power is an interesting concept. Too often we can point to individuals and groups throughout history who have misused their power resulting in brutalization, subjugation, and annihilation. Sometimes just the word itself makes us feel uncomfortable, and we yearn to develop ourselves and our society with words like *nurture*, *facilitate*, *encourage*, and *foster*. However, if we consider the root of the word, which comes from the French *poeir* (to be able), we can see how the seemingly kinder words depend upon the power of the individual to be able to accomplish the actions the words describe. Ideas and information are the essential ingredients for power, and the extent to which we are able to help our students become powerful by learning how to use these ingredients effectively—to help them to become information literate—determines the quality of their future and that of our global society.

Helen Thompson and Susan Henley have provided us with a wonderful blueprint that is firmly based on theory and well grounded in practice. This is such a critical aspect of our efforts as library media specialists attempting to make change happen in our schools. Our individual opinions are important, especially if they have been developed through some systematic process of inquiry. At the same time, if we want teachers, principals, boards, and parents to listen to our opinions, we must be able to show them how we came to believe what we believe. Most important, we must be able to show *why* adherence to our beliefs will ensure student achievement. Helen and Susan practice what they preach, and they have provided you with an invaluable guide to help you accomplish change in your school. The change we want is not only to create a positive impact with teachers and parents concerning our images as instructional partners but also to create a positive impact on the lives of the next generation. If we want to ensure that these next generations will have the power to be productive citizens in a democratic society that values the individual as well as the mosaic of cultures, we have to help them become information literate. As Helen and Susan point out so well, this means that we need to help them become thinkers in the deepest sense of the word. We must foster our students' powers so that they will take responsibility for their own learning: They will not be satisfied with just answers, but will always ask questions.

The mark of my success and the pride of practice in my job are best summarized in the old saying: May the student exceed the teacher. It has been my pleasure to work with Helen and Susan in their academic endeavors and to see them exceed this teacher. I believe that you will find their work an important resource in helping you craft an information literacy program that will result in the enjoyment of your students' success.

Dan Barron
Columbia, SC
1999

NOTES

1.   Michael Riordan and Lillian Hoddeson, *Crystal Fire: The Birth of the Information Age* (New York: Norton, 1997), 285.

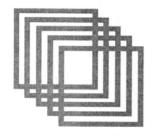

Preface

BACKGROUND AND PURPOSE
OF THE BOOK

This book began with the question: What would you need to implement information literacy instruction in your school? After much thought, we decided we would need to know just what information literacy is, why it is important, how it can be measured, who would be responsible for teaching it, and when and where it should be taught. The initial what, why, and how of information literacy are included, for the most part, in the various information literacy standards developed by states and organizations (see chapters 1, 2, and 4). Additional research revealed the who, when, and where. For information literacy instruction to be most effective, all members of the faculty should be responsible for it, and it should be taught throughout all curriculum areas in both the classroom and the library media center (see chapter 5).

So far, so good. Now we knew. But our teachers didn't. In order to implement information literacy instruction in our school, we needed a way to inform our teachers and persuade them to participate, so we developed an in-service presentation and handout (appendix F). We wanted to convince teachers that information literacy is not "something extra" to be taught in addition to their normal curriculum but is an attitude, a process, a way of thinking that can be introduced and encouraged while subject matter is being learned. To do this, we included background information, explanations, articles, and links to national curriculum guidelines (chapter 3 and appendixes A, B, C, D, and E). We wanted to share what we learned about the process of problem solving—how it is the essence of intelligence and an essential component of information literacy—so we added a bit about heuristics and how they could be used with students (chapter 6).

We had to make it easy for our colleagues to plan cooperatively with each other and with us and keep track of what was being taught. Therefore, we developed the checklist of information literacy skills (chapter 8). To help teachers put it all together, we included information about designing information literacy lessons for all types of students (chapter 7). Finally, because we wanted to give concrete examples of information literacy in action, we designed lesson plans that encouraged researching, thinking, evaluating, and communicating (chapter 9).

We deliberated over a title for our project, considering and then rejecting *Teaching Information Literacy* and *Ensuring Information Literacy*. Information literacy, we learned, is not just an assortment of skills that can be taught, and no amount of teaching will ensure that students will become information literate. Each person—each student—must accept the responsibility for his or her own information literacy. But, as educators, we can and should expose students to the concepts of information literacy and encourage and facilitate the process of acquiring, evaluating, using, and communicating knowledge and ideas. Thus, we finally settled on our title: *Fostering Information Literacy*.

We enjoyed our journey—our exploration into the subject of information literacy. We hope you enjoy yours!

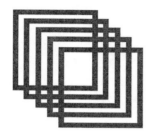 # Acknowledgments

We wish to thank the following:

Dr. Daniel D. Barron for starting us on this path and advising us along the way; Dr. Paula Montgomery for helping us through the initial process, connecting us with the right people, and encouraging our efforts; the faculties of Edmund A. Burns Elementary School and Haut Gap Middle School (many of the ideas for lesson plans and scenarios came from teachers, and their inspiration was the groundwork for many other ideas in this book); Polly Greene (library media specialist), Andi Jordan and Ann Malone from James Island Middle School for their help with the Inventions unit; our editor, Betty Morris, for her kind help and support; and, of course, our families, who put up with us and encouraged us through the whole process.

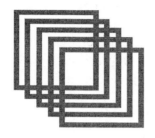

CHAPTER 1

What Is Information Literacy?

What one knows is, in youth, of little moment;
they know enough who know how to learn.

—Henry Brooks Adams

THE DEFINITION

What is information literacy? Although it is a relatively modern term, Henry Brooks Adams recognized it more than ninety years ago. He expressed the concept of information literacy when he said, "they know enough who know how to learn." Information literacy is knowing how to learn. It is knowing how to find information, evaluate it, and use it wisely and effectively. Adams knew that we don't always remember everything we learn when we are young (and in school); some things are not relevant to our later lives. Adams also probably knew that we can't possibly learn everything we will need to know later while we are still in school. We have to know how to learn—to be lifelong learners.

The term *literacy* traditionally has meant the ability to read, or to derive meaning from words. *Information literacy* translates into the ability to derive meaning from information, or "the ability to access, evaluate and use information from a variety of sources."[1] Another expert calls it the fourth R, *Reasoning*. He contends that, during this time when information is our most important resource, Reasoning (or information literacy) will ward off information anxiety by helping students make sense out of the glut of information that surrounds them.[2]

Information literacy demands skills more complex than the traditional library skills that have been taught for years; it requires more thought than simply finding a source and copying the information for a report. Information literacy skills include recognizing when information is needed, selecting appropriate sources from the overwhelming amount of available print and nonprint resources, evaluating the information for accuracy and pertinence, organizing the facts so that they make sense, creating knowledge by associating the new information with previous knowledge and experiences, and then using this knowledge wisely. Other essential skills contained in the concept of information literacy are problem solving, critical thinking, creative thinking, recognizing patterns, understanding relationships, and transferring knowledge from one discipline or setting to another. All of these are abilities that enable the learner to derive meaning from information—to learn to learn. Information literacy also implies a self-motivated enjoyment of learning and a responsibility to contribute to and abide by the rules of our information society and our community of learners.

Information-literate people do not necessarily know a lot of facts. However, they do know how to find the answers or solve the problems. Their knowledge base includes information resources, search strategies, evaluation tips, organizing skills, and problem-solving processes that span all curriculum subjects and ultimately are more valuable than specific facts.

> *Alice doesn't know (or remember) the capitals of all the states or where they are located on a map, but she does know what sources have that information if she ever needs it. More important, she has the skills to plan a vacation or a business trip. She knows how to read an atlas or map, chart a route from place A to place B, estimate the number of days it will take to drive it, and identify places to stay along the way. She also can develop a budget, determine the costs for other transportation methods, and then decide whether she wants to drive, fly, or take the train or bus.*

Information-literate people know *how* to learn and they use their knowledge wisely.

CHARACTERISTICS OF AN INFORMATION-LITERATE PERSON

People who are information literate possess other skills and share other characteristics. In addition to being able to access, evaluate, and use information wisely, they also enjoy reading and learning about things that are important to them. They seek information to satisfy personal needs or interests. They observe copyright laws and respect intellectual freedom. They participate cooperatively in groups, respect others' contributions and viewpoints, and willingly share their own knowledge. They are creative thinkers and problem solvers and recognize that there is not always one right answer to every question. They see patterns, not just in things or events but also in ideas, concepts, and actions, and they use these insights to predict outcomes or make decisions. They can apply a skill learned in one discipline or setting to other subjects and to new situations. They connect new information to their previous experiences and knowledge, changing or modifying their own perceptions and opinions as necessary. They can interpret graphs, charts, and maps and derive meaning from art, music, dance, and drama. They analyze and critique their own work—their research processes, information findings, and communication products—regularly formulating strategies and methods for improvement. Most important, they experience the joy of learning and are lifelong learners.

In the publication *Information Literacy in an Information Society: A Concept for the Information Age*, Christina S. Doyle describes an information-literate person as one who

- recognizes that accurate and complete knowledge is the basis for intelligent decision making;

- recognizes the need for information;

- formulates questions based on information needs;

- identifies potential sources of information;

- develops successful search strategies;

- accesses sources of information including computer-based and other technologies;

- evaluates information;

- organizes information for practical application;

- integrates new information into an existing body of knowledge; and

- uses information in critical thinking and problem solving.[3]

These characteristics are part of the foundation of the information literacy movement. Many of the later works concerning information literacy build upon Doyle's definition and her characteristics of an information-literate person.

PUBLISHED STANDARDS AND STATEMENTS

Several states and educational organizations have developed information literacy guidelines or standards. These standards are intended to be used in all curriculum areas and by teachers in the classroom as well as by media specialists in the library. Although most of them contain the same basic components, there are some differences.

Colorado

Colorado's Department of Education's *Model of Information Literacy Guidelines* depicts information-literate students as those who are 1) knowledge seekers, 2) quality producers, 3) self-directed learners, 4) group contributors, and 5) responsible information users. The first guideline is important because the process of seeking knowledge is something that must be taught and learned. Because the process of seeking knowledge usually results in some kind of product, the first two guidelines are connected. The third guideline concerns the significance of independent learning, which ultimately produces a "lifelong learner." The fourth guideline is relevant because we are a society and must learn to function in groups. The last guideline is important because responsibility and ethical behavior go hand in hand. These models of information literacy are deliberately called "guidelines" instead of "standards." The Colorado Information Literacy Advisory Committee does not want the guidelines to be considered as content-area standards, but rather as processes for learning that could and should be integrated within the different content areas.[4]

Wisconsin

The Wisconsin Educational Media Association also offers a set of standards for information literacy. Their standards are called *Information Problem-Solving Skills*. The seven skills are 1) defining information need, 2) initiating search strategies, 3) locating resources, 4) assessing and comprehending information, 5) interpreting and 6) communicating the information, and finally, 7) evaluating the process and product. These seven areas focus on research skills and go into great detail for each skill. They do not mention the information literacy components that are concerned with students as independent or ethical learners.[5]

Vermont

The guidelines from the state of Vermont are similar to those of Wisconsin's. However, Vermont relates their standards with their *Framework of Standards and Learning Opportunities*. They also stress the paramount importance of making information literacy a school-wide effort.[6]

California

The state of California focuses on similar traits in their *Essential Components of Information Literacy* document. Once again, the emphasis seems to be on the research process. The characteristics of students as independent learners and as responsible and ethical citizens are not addressed.[7]

Griffith University

Griffith University in Brisbane, Australia, has developed an *Information Literacy Blueprint* to further information literacy instruction for students and faculty. The *Blueprint* quotes Christina Doyle's definition and abilities of an information-literate person and lists seven characteristics of the information-literate person:

1. engages in independent, self-directed learning

2. implements information processes

3. uses a variety of information technologies and systems

4. internalizes values which promote information use

5. has a sound knowledge of the world of information

6. approaches information critically

7. has a personal information style which facilitates his or her interaction with the world of information.[8]

Although the *Blueprint* was developed for a university, the information literacy characteristics listed can apply to elementary students as well as learners of all ages.

National Forum on Information Literacy

The National Forum on Information Literacy (NFIL) is a group of organizations concerned with information literacy education. The Association for Supervision and Curriculum Development (ASCD), a highly respected educational organization, is a member of this national forum. The group defines information-literate students as those who:

> can successfully complete a complex problem-solving process that requires them to define the need for information, determine a search strategy, locate the needed resources, assess and understand the information they find, interpret the information, communicate the information, and, finally, evaluate their conclusions in view of the original problem.[9]

AASL/AECT

The American Association of School Librarians (AASL) and the Association for Educational Communications and Technology (AECT) provide a list of information literacy standards that divide the characteristics of an information-literate person into three categories: Information Literacy, Independent Learning, and Social Responsibility. These categories are subdivided into nine standards that are defined by twenty-nine indicators. The Information Literacy Standards specify the abilities needed to access, evaluate, and use information critically and wisely. The Independent Learning Standards list the characteristics of a self-motivated, lifelong learner. The final set of standards, Social Responsibility, emphasizes teamwork and respect for copyright laws and intellectual freedom.[10] The standards further subdivide these broad information literacy skills into specific demonstrable abilities or indicators. The indicators are extremely helpful to teachers and library media specialists because they stipulate the skills that need to be taught, emphasized, modeled, and practiced to foster information literacy in students. They become measurable objectives for unit and lesson plans, and offer criteria for evaluating students' progress and performance. These standards and indicators are the frameworks for building an information literacy curriculum for school-wide use. This book is designed to support the AASL/AECT information literacy standards and offers suggestions for their implementation through a fully integrated, school-wide information literacy program. The Information Literacy Standards for Student Learning are reproduced as they are found in *Information Power: Building Partnerships for Learning*.

The AASL/AECT Standards

Information Literacy Standards

Standard 1:   *The student who is information literate accesses information efficiently and effectively.*

Indicators:

1. recognizes the need for information;

2. recognizes that accurate and comprehensive information is the basis for intelligent decision making;

3. formulates questions based on information needs;

4. identifies a variety of potential sources of information;

5. develops and uses successful strategies for locating information.

Standard 2:   *The student who is information literate evaluates information critically and competently.*

Indicators:

1. determines accuracy, relevance, and comprehensiveness;

2. distinguishes among fact, point of view, and opinion;

3. identifies inaccurate and misleading information;

4. selects information appropriate to the problem or question at hand.

Standard 3:   *The student who is information literate uses information accurately and creatively.*

Indicators:

1. organizes information for practical application;

2. integrates new information into one's own knowledge;

3. applies information in critical thinking and problem solving;

4. produces and communicates information and ideas in appropriate formats.

Independent Learning Standards

Standard 4:   *The student who is an independent learner is information literate and pursues information related to personal interests.*

Indicators:

1. seeks information related to various dimensions of personal well-being, such as career interests, community involvement, health matters, and recreational pursuits;

2. designs, develops, and evaluates information products and solutions related to personal interests.

Standard 5:   *The student who is an independent learner is information literate and appreciates literature and other creative expressions of information.*

Indicators:

1. is a competent and self-motivated reader;

2. derives meaning from information presented creatively in a variety of formats;

3. develops creative products in a variety of formats.

Standard 6:   *The student who is an independent learner is information literate and strives for excellence in information seeking and knowledge generation.*

Indicators:

1. assesses the quality of the process and products of one's own information seeking;

2. devises strategies for revising, improving, and updating self-generated knowledge.

Social Responsibility Standards

Standard 7:   *The student who contributes positively to the learning community and to society is information literate and recognizes the importance of information to a democratic society.*

Indicators:

1. seeks information from diverse sources, contexts, disciplines, and cultures;

2. respects the principle of equitable access to information.

Standard 8: *The student who contributes positively to the learning community and to society is information literate and practices ethical behavior in regard to information and information technology.*

Indicators:

1. respects the principles of intellectual freedom;

2. respects intellectual property rights;

3. uses information technology responsibly.

Standard 9: *The student who contributes positively to the learning community and to society is information literate and participates effectively in groups to pursue and generate information.*

Indicators:

1. shares knowledge and information with others;

2. respects others' ideas and backgrounds and acknowledges their contributions;

3. collaborates with others, both in person and through technologies, to identify information problems and to seek their solutions;

4. collaborates with others, both in person and through technologies, to design, develop, and evaluate information products and solutions.

IN OTHER WORDS . . . INTERPRETING THE STANDARDS

Information Literacy Standards

An information-literate person is one who knows how to learn by efficiently accessing, critically evaluating, and effectively using information for academic and personal reasons (standards 1, 2, 3). These indicators are similar to the standards developed by other states and organizations: They indicate the steps of the research process. These steps are the thought processes and activities information-literate learners use when faced with a problem or an information need. The main components, as indicated in the Information Literacy Standards, are recognizing a need for information, asking appropriate questions, identifying potential resources, developing search strategies, evaluating the information for accuracy and relevancy, organizing the information, and using it to answer the question or to solve the problem. Although it is listed here and in the other standards in a linear form with one step following another, the actual process is not necessarily an ordered progression. The research process and some published models are discussed in more detail in chapter 4.

Amy wanted to give her mother a special birthday present. A class unit on plants gave her an idea. She knew her mother liked flowers, so she decided to give her mother a small flower garden. Her teacher suggested that she use the flower garden as her unit project. Amy thought about what she would need to know when selecting and planting the flowers. She had learned the difference between perennials and annuals and wanted to choose some of each. She obtained information about the different flowers and about soil preparation from books, Web sites, gardening magazines, and a government extension agency. The library media specialist noticed that Amy was having trouble organizing all her information, so she showed her how to create a database with Flower Name, Perennial or Annual, Sun or Shade, Blooming Season, Type of Soil, Climate, and Color as field names. With the information clearly organized, Amy was able to sort and select varieties that would grow well in her climate, bloom at different times of the year, and provide an assortment of color. She planted the garden and gave her mother a booklet with the names and pictures of all the plants and what she could expect each season. Her mother loved the present. When Amy told her teacher and classmates about it, they liked the idea so much that they decided to plan and plant a garden at school.

Amy used information literacy skills to define an information need, to select resources, to research and organize her information, and to use it appropriately.

Independent Learning Standards

An independent learner is a self-motivated learner—one who is information literate and who seeks information to satisfy personal needs and interests. These needs and interests may be related to career or health concerns, to hobbies or commitments (standard 4).

> *Lisa is concerned about the diminishing wetlands. She gathers information about wetland conservation, then repackages and distributes it to civic groups, businesses, and governmental offices.*
>
> *Scott is undecided about his career. He fills in personal interest and abilities surveys, identifies interesting career clusters, and visits professionals in those fields. He completes college and scholarship applications and drafts resumes for part-time jobs.*
>
> *Deni has just been diagnosed with juvenile diabetes. In the hospital, she reads pamphlets, watches videos, and talks with doctors, nurses, and dietitians. She learns how to manage her disease to stay healthy and live an active life. Back at school, she presents a slide show to her classmates explaining juvenile diabetes, its symptoms, and the available treatments.*
>
> *Dan likes to cook. He collects recipes from his relatives and combines them into a cookbook. He includes family legends that he has researched and tales from past gatherings; he gives the books out at the next family reunion.*

Lisa, Scott, Deni, and Dan are information literate, self-motivated, independent learners.

An independent learner also appreciates and derives meaning from a variety of formats: books and plays, art and dance, poetry and music (standard 5).

> *Sally loves to read. She reads fiction, nonfiction, and poetry. She acts out the stories in her books and draws pictures illustrating her favorite poems.*

> *Steven listens to the music of the Civil War and feels the sadness and melancholy of an army camp.*
>
> *Bill studies the colorful photographs of birds on the poster in his room and identifies some of the birds that visit the feeder in his back yard. He photographs the birds not pictured on the poster and creates his own chart for his family to use.*

These students are information-literate independent learners as well.

Another characteristic of the independent learner is the desire to improve searching techniques and finished products (standard 6). This desire is accomplished by regular assessment and evaluation of the information searches and products. If the search is not going well, an information-literate, independent learner takes stock, determines the problem, and adapts the strategy. If the quality of the product is not satisfactory, the independent learner seeks to improve it, learning new skills if necessary.

> *Sarah is researching national parks for vacation ideas, but is overwhelmed with the amount of information she finds. She decides to concentrate her search on just the few states closest to her own. This revision of her search strategy limits the information she receives, enabling Sarah to deal with it and to focus on what is most relevant for her.*

Sarah is an information-literate, independent learner.

Social Responsibility Standards

The third category of the AASL/AECT standards concerns the social responsibility of an information-literate person. In a community of learners, an information-literate person contributes positively by participating in groups, respecting copyright laws, observing the principles of intellectual freedom, allowing others access to information, appreciating the information contributions of various cultures and disciplines, and sharing his or her knowledge with others (standards 7, 8, 9).

> *Patricia demonstrates social responsibility when she cites the information sources she used in a report on guinea pigs. Philip acts responsibly when he refuses to make a copy of a computer game for a friend. Ed and Anne contribute positively when they work together to determine the amount of pollution in the harbor and then post that information on the Internet.*

Information literacy and society are interdependent; to survive in our ever-changing world, students need to become information literate. The proliferation of new and unregulated information that surrounds us is mind-boggling. Students must be able to identify, access, evaluate, and use that information wisely. The world, in turn, depends upon information-literate people for its survival. These people must be willing to respect others and their opinions, to communicate and collaborate with others, and to share their knowledge with those who will benefit from it.

> *Ms. Black's students show social responsibility when they work together to collect data on the migration of birds through their community and report this information (via e-mail) to the university professor who is coordinating the research project from a neighboring state.*

Ms. Black's students are socially responsible, information-literate people.

SUMMARY

Information literacy is the ability to learn or to derive meaning from information, to think, and to reason. People who are information literate recognize an information need, know where and how to find information, evaluate and select relevant information, organize their findings to suit their needs, and use this new information effectively. They are both independent learners and group participants. They observe copyright laws and respect the information rights and opinions of others. Information-literate people are empowered by their ability to absorb new information, to solve problems, and to adapt to new situations. Information literacy standards have been developed by several states and organizations and may be used as guidelines for teaching and fostering information literacy.

NOTES

1.   C. S. Doyle, *Information Literacy in an Information Society: A Concept for the Information Age* (Syracuse, NY: ERIC Clearinghouse on Information and Technology, 1994), 1. Reprinted by permission. This publication gives the most widely used definition of information literacy along with a history of the use of the term. Doyle also relates information literacy to national education goals, the SCANS Report, and national subject curriculum standards. Included is an annotated ERIC bibliography of information literacy resources.

2.   Daniel D. Barron, *Information Literacy R Basic* (Columbia, SC: University of South Carolina, College of Library and Information Science, unpublished manuscript, November 1997). Used with permission. Barron offers his reason for calling information literacy the fourth R (knowledge of information is just as critical and basic as knowledge of

the other three Rs) and tells of the development of the AASL/AECT Information Literacy Standards. He reviews recent research on the subject and includes an annotated bibliography.

3.   Doyle, 3. Referred to as an expanded definition of information literacy, or what it means to be information literate, Doyle's list of characteristics is also widely used and is the basis for many of the information literacy standards. They were originally published in 1992 in Doyle's *Final Report to National Forum on Information Literacy.*

4.   Dian Walster and Lynda Welborn, "Colorado's Information Literacy Guidelines," *School Library Media Activities Monthly* 12 no. 7 (1996), 23–27. Reprinted by permission. This article introduces Colorado's *Guidelines* by explaining their development and why they are deliberately called guidelines rather than standards. It describes each of the five guidelines in detail and ends with an adaptation of the guidelines written specifically for middle school students in language they can understand. The official guideline site is http://cde.state.co.us/infolitg.htm (see Additional Readings).

5.   Wisconsin Educational Media Association, 1993, *Information Literacy: A Position Paper on Information Problem-Solving.* URL: http://www.marshfield.k12.wi.us/wema/infolit.html. (Accessed November 8, 1999). Reprinted by permission. This site introduces the concept of information literacy, discusses the necessary restructuring of schools, and describes an effective information literacy curriculum. The Information Problem-Solving Skills are listed and are followed by three scenarios of information literacy in action. This position paper has been adopted and reprinted with permission by the American Association of School Librarians (see Additional Readings).

6.   Vermont Department of Education, 1996, *Information Literacy for Vermont Students: A Planning Guide.* URL: http://www.vema.together.com/infolit.htm. (Accessed November 9, 1999). Reprinted by permission. This planning guide includes a foreword concerning the reasons for and process of developing the document, a statement on equity and access to information, the list of information literacy standards, primary, middle, and high school scenarios, and helpful rubrics for evaluating information processing.

7.   Information Literacy Task Force, Region VII California Technology Assistance Project, 1998. *Information Literacy: Guidelines for Kindergarten Through Grade 12.* URL: http://ctap.fcoe.k12.ca.us/ctap/Info.Lit/infolit.html. (Accessed November 8, 1999). Reprinted by permission. This is one of the most comprehensive and useful information literacy sites. It includes sections on the importance of information literacy, essential components of information literacy, a graphic illustration of the organized investigator, a chart of the developmental stages of an information-literate student, types of collaborative units of instruction, and links to other information literacy sites.

8. Christine Susan Bruce, 1994, *Information Literacy Blueprint*. URL: http://www. gu.edu.au/ins/lils/infolit/blueprint/blueprnt.htm. (Accessed November 8, 1999). Reprinted by permission of Griffith University. Valuable for its use as a planning model, the *Information Literacy Blueprint* is divided into two sections: a theoretical framework and a strategic plan. The theoretical framework discusses the characteristics of an information-literate person, information literacy education, and the different roles of those involved. The strategic plan outlines strategies for information literacy core education, staff development, curriculum development, and extracurricular education. Included in appendix 1 is an interesting chart comparing different aspects of the "Long Standing View of Learning" to the "Emerging View of Learning."

9. Philip Cohen, "Developing Information Literacy," *Education Update* 37 no. 2 (1995), 1, 3, 8. Reprinted with permission from ASCD. All rights reserved. This article gives a brief reason for promoting information literacy, offers a practical method of implementation (resource-based learning), outlines the new teacher and library media specialists' roles this demands, and discusses some of the common hurdles that are in the way of information literacy instruction. It can be found at http://www.ascd.org/pubs/eu/feb95.html. (Accessed November 8, 1999).

10. From *Information Power: Building Partnerships for Learning* by American Association of School Libraries and Association for Educational Communications and Technology. Copyright © 1998 American Library Association for Educational Communications and Technology. Reprinted by permission of the American Library Association. This publication includes Information Literacy Standards for Student Learning, which is the source of the information literacy standards used in this book.

ADDITIONAL READINGS

Information Literacy

Information Literacy. URL: http://inst.augie.edu/~asmith/infolit.html. Accessed November 8, 1999. Written by an Augustana Public Services/Reference Librarian, this interesting and sometimes humorous site discusses information anxiety, defines information literacy, lists the abilities of an information-literate person, offers personal observations about information-illiterate students, and concludes with eight principles of teaching and learning skill development that may be applied to the teaching of information literacy skills. Links provide the symptoms of information anxiety, a short description of the "Information Frankenstein," synonyms for information literacy, an exercise in problem solving, suggestions for teaching students how to evaluate sources and understand bibliographies, and connections to other information literacy topics.

Position Statement on Information Literacy: A Position Paper on Information Problem Solving. 1996. URL: http://ala.org/aasl/positions/ps_infolit.html. Accessed November 8, 1999. This is a reprint of the *Position Paper* developed by the Wisconsin Educational Media Association. The AASL Web site concludes with eight scenarios of information literacy in action, written by Paula Montgomery, editor of *School Library Media Activities Monthly.*

Information Literacy Standards

North Carolina Department of Public Instruction. 1995. *Information Skills Curriculum: Competency Goals.* URL: http://www.dpi.state.nc.us/Curriculum/Information/c_goals.htm. Accessed November 8, 1999. This Web site lists two competency goals for the *Information Skills Curriculum*: 1) "The learner will experience a wide variety of reading, listening, and viewing resources to interact with ideas in an information-intensive environment" and 2) "The learner will identify and apply strategies to access, evaluate, use, and communicate information for learning, decision making, and problem solving." A more detailed description is provided for both. It is stressed that these skills will enable students to become lifelong learners and informed decision makers. The site includes links to the *Advisory List of Instructional Technology.*

Washington Library Media Association. 1996. *Essential Skills for Information Literacy.* URL: http://www.wlma.org/literacy/eslintro.htm. Accessed November 8, 1999. Developed in 1996 by the Office of the Superintendent of Public Instruction, Olympia, Washington, and the Washington Library Media Association, this document is intended to be used as a guide for individual schools and districts as they plan their local curriculum. The *Essential Skills and Components* section focuses on the research process: 1) recognizing a need for information; 2) constructing strategies for locating information; 3) locating and accessing information; 4) evaluating and extracting information; 5) organizing and applying information; and 6) evaluating the process and product. The *Guiding Principles* section includes a "Statement by Commission on Student Learning," which gives an excellent description of information literacy skills and abilities needed by today's students and also stresses the responsibility of the schools to provide this instruction. The site provides links to sites that specify benchmarks for the components of each skill.

CHAPTER **2**

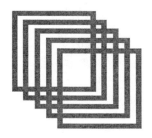

Why Information Literacy?

Knowledge is power.
—Francis Bacon

Why should we teach information literacy skills and foster information-literate attitudes? We should because, as educators, we agree with Francis Bacon: Knowledge is power. But what kind of knowledge is most powerful today? At one time, knowledge of a trade was powerful enough to earn a living and ensure success. Later, the three Rs (Reading, 'Riting, and 'Rithmetic) were considered more powerful. Today, in an age of abundant good, bad, and ever-changing information, knowledge of information itself is the most powerful. Knowing how to find, understand, manage, use, and respect information empowers students and boosts their success in academics, in the workforce, and in their personal lives.

Society recognizes that knowledge of information (information literacy) is a valuable and powerful tool. Educational organizations stress it in their mission statements, national laws mandate it for future citizens, businesses require it of their workers, and students and people of all ages benefit from it for both academic and personal reasons. The following sections of this chapter are devoted to justifying information literacy instruction in today's schools by highlighting the connections between information literacy and national educational goals and concerns.

INFORMATION POWER

School library media specialists should foster and encourage information literacy instruction because it is our professional duty; it is our mission. In *Information Power: Building Partnerships for Learning* (1998), the American Library Association says the mission of the library media program is "to ensure that all students and staff are effective users of knowledge and ideas."[1] Effective users of knowledge and ideas know how to access and evaluate information. They share information by communicating and collaborating with others. Finally, they use their knowledge and ideas effectively to solve problems or to make decisions. Accessing, evaluating, sharing, and using information are all information literacy skills or abilities. In other words, the mission of library media programs is to teach and foster information literacy instruction.

GOALS 2000

Library media specialists are not the only educators who should be concerned with information literacy instruction. The information literacy standards advocated by the American Association of School Librarians and other educational state departments and organizations are reiterated in the Goals 2000: Educate America Act, passed by Congress in 1996. This act seeks to improve learning and teaching by promoting educational research and reform and by developing national standards for student achievement and teacher certification. The main educational goals for the year 2000 emphasize:

1. School Readiness

2. School Completion

3. Student Achievement and Citizenship

4. Teacher Education and Professional Development

5. Mathematics and Science

6. Adult Literacy and Lifelong Learning

7. Safe, Disciplined, and Alcohol- and Drug-Free Schools

8. Parental Participation[2]

Two of these goals, "Student Achievement and Citizenship" and "Adult Literacy and Lifelong Learning," depend upon information literacy skills for their fulfillment. Three others, "School Readiness," "School Completion," and "Parental Participation," will be achieved through the same educational reforms and strategies needed to foster information literacy.

Part of Goal 3, "Student Achievement and Citizenship," states that "By the year 2000 . . . every school in America will ensure that all students learn to use their minds well, so they may be prepared for responsible citizenship, further learning, and productive employment in our Nation's modern economy."[3] The Objectives ii, iii, and vi relate to information literacy. They read as follows:

Goal 3, Objective ii: The percentage of all students who demonstrate the ability to reason, solve problems, apply knowledge, and write and communicate effectively will increase substantially;

Goal 3, Objective iii: All students will be involved in activities that promote and demonstrate good citizenship, good health, community service, and personal responsibility;

Goal 3, Objective vi: All students will be knowledgeable about the diverse cultural heritage of this Nation and about the world community.[4]

A student who demonstrates the ability to reason, solve problems, apply knowledge, and write and communicate effectively *is* information literate. These abilities are essential information literacy skills and are stated or implied in all information literacy standards. They are defined in the AASL/AECT Standards and Indicators as accessing, evaluating, and using information (standards 1, 2, 3).

Good citizenship and personal responsibility are also information literacy characteristics. The AASL/AECT Standards list these attributes as Social Responsibility Standards. The indicators stress group participation, adherence to copyright laws, and respect for intellectual freedom (standards 7, 8, 9). Those responsible for the Goals 2000 document also realized that for our students to participate fully in a democratic society they must learn to become "responsible" citizens. To become informed participants, citizens must be able to distinguish between fact and opinion, research and advertisement. With all the information available today, this ability to determine the truth has become increasingly difficult. The information literacy skills of evaluation and critical thinking are necessary for this task.

Objective vi of Goal 3 is related because the information literacy standards emphasize the value of seeking information from diverse cultures and respecting and appreciating differences in thoughts and ideas. In the process of seeking information from other cultures, students will become knowledgeable about them and their contributions to the world community.

Goal 6, "Adult Literacy and Lifelong Learning," states: "By the year 2000, every adult American will be literate and will possess the knowledge and skills necessary to compete in a global economy and exercise the rights and responsibilities of citizenship."[5] The specific objectives that apply to information literacy are:

Goal 6, Objective ii: All workers will have the opportunity to acquire the knowledge and skills, from basic to highly technical, needed to adapt to emerging new technologies, work methods, and markets.

Goal 6, Objective v: The proportion of college students who demonstrate an advanced ability to think critically, communicate effectively, and solve problems will increase substantially.[6]

Information literacy skills enable students, workers, and everyone else to learn new information and to adapt to new situations. Recognizing the need for information, identifying potential sources, connecting new information to old knowledge, and transferring knowledge from one setting to another are some of the basic concepts of information literacy. Knowing how to learn empowers and benefits everyone. Thinking critically, communicating effectively, and solving problems are also essential concepts of information literacy. These competencies cannot be taught and learned during just four years of college. To be effective, these skills must be introduced, taught, and fostered throughout the school years and beyond.

Other Goals 2000 objectives also are supported by information literacy instruction. Both Goals 2000 and information literacy programs acknowledge that parents are their children's first teachers; as such, they are responsible for helping their children to learn. Specific responsibilities of parents in fostering information literacy are discussed further in chapter 5, but those outlined in Goals 2000 include preparing children to learn, supporting schools, and holding teachers accountable to high standards (Goal 8, Parental Participation, Objective iii). Information literacy instruction represents the highest standards and the highest order of thinking skills in all curriculum areas.

SCANS REPORT

Another national document that supports information literacy instruction is the *Secretary's Commission on Achieving Necessary Skills (SCANS) Report*. This document identifies three fundamental foundations and five competencies necessary for tomorrow's workforce. The thinking skills included in the three-part foundation are:

A. Creative Thinking—generates new ideas

B. Decision Making—specifies goals and constraints, generates alternatives, considers risks, and evaluates and chooses best alternative

C. Problem Solving—recognizes problems and devises and implements plan of action

D. Seeing Things in the Mind's Eye—organizes and processes symbols, pictures, graphs, objects, and other information

E. Knowing How to Learn—uses efficient learning techniques to acquire and apply new knowledge and skills

F. Reasoning—discovers a rule or principle underlying the relationship between two or more objects and applies it in solving a problem[7]

These "thinking skills" are information literacy skills either stated or implied as indicators of the AASL/AECT Information Literacy Standards for Student Learning.

The *SCANS Report* requires that future workers are competent in five areas: Resources, Interpersonal, Information, Systems, and Technology. The Interpersonal, Information, and Technology areas are directly related to information literacy. According to the report, the Interpersonal competencies needed are

A. Participates As Member of a Team—contributes to group effort

B. Teaches Others New Skills—serves as instructor

C. Serves Clients/Customers—relates to those outside the workplace

D. Exercises Leadership—communicates ideas to justify position, persuades and convinces others, responsibly challenges existing procedures and policies

E. Negotiates—compromises when necessary

F. Works with Diversity—works well with men and women from diverse backgrounds (*SCANS Report*, Interpersonal Skills)

Group participation, sharing knowledge and information with others, communicating ideas, and respecting others' opinions or ideas are all information literacy goals and objectives.

The *SCANS Report* states that a worker who exhibits competency with information

A. Acquires and Evaluates Information

B. Organizes and Maintains Information

C. Interprets and Communicates Information

D. Uses Computers to Process Information (*SCANS Report*, Information Skills)

These competencies are listed specifically as indicators in the Information Literacy Standards.

The third SCANS competency characterizes a worker who is competent with technology as one who "works with a variety of technologies" or

A. Selects Technology—chooses procedures, tools, or equipment including computers and related technologies

B. Applies Technology to Task—understands overall intent and proper procedures for setup and operation of equipment

C. Maintains and Troubleshoots Equipment—prevents, identifies, or solves problems with equipment, including computers and other technologies (*SCANS Report*, Technology Skills)

Information literacy requires the ability to obtain information from a variety of formats, including computer or other technology-based resources. It also involves the ability to create information products (i.e., choosing the most appropriate format for the audience and the task). The close alignment of information literacy skills to the SCANS skills necessary for future workers is one more justification for fostering information literacy instruction in today's schools.

SUBJECT-AREA CONTENT STANDARDS

Information literacy skills can and should be taught throughout all curriculum areas because they reiterate some of the same skills incorporated in national, state, and local curriculum standards. All subject areas now stress critical-thinking and problem-solving abilities. Most emphasize research skills as well. These are all skills that are taught and fostered through information literacy instruction. Chapter 3 goes into greater detail about the relationship between information literacy standards and subject-area content standards, and the appendixes include charts illustrating the similarities.

STANDARDIZED TESTS

Although their use remains a highly debated issue, standardized tests are still a fact of life in most schools. Raising standardized test scores has become a national priority, and teachers are continuously testing new programs and instructional methods that claim to accomplish this task. We recommend school-wide information literacy instruction as a strategy to increase student learning and understanding, thereby increasing student test scores. There are several reasons for this recommendation: First, standardized tests no longer measure just students' knowledge of facts but also measure students' knowledge of processes and procedures. A typical procedural question might be, "How can you find out what a cocoon is?" Information literacy instruction stresses all the skills involved in accessing information, including identifying resources and developing search strategies. Standardized tests measure students' problem-solving abilities as well. Using information in critical thinking and problem solving is another major information literacy component. The tests also require students to interpret information from graphs and charts. Information literacy skills include the ability to derive information from a variety of formats. Some test questions may be open-ended and require written answers. Others may have "Not Given" as one of the answer choices. These kinds of questions require thinking skills, not memorization skills.[8] Information literacy is the ability to think and to reason well.

These justifications, however sound and valid, imply a "teaching to the test" mentality. Therefore, we offer a more honorable one: Information literacy instruction promotes researching and understanding information, not just memorizing facts. It emphasizes critical-thinking and reasoning skills and ensures that students have learned how to learn. Just as students who can think and reason and know how to learn will succeed in school and in later life, students who can think, reason, and learn, and can explain those processes, will succeed on standardized tests.

AT-RISK STUDENTS

Information literacy skills benefit students in their everyday academics as well as on standardized tests and in their future jobs and careers. Students who have mastered information literacy skills have an easier time with assignments and projects; they know where to begin asking questions and how to start finding answers. Although all students profit from information literacy instruction, for some students it can be critical for success. At-risk students are defined as being at risk of failing, for a variety of reasons.[9] For these students, school has been a very unpleasant experience and unless that changes, they are likely to quit before graduation. Recent research on effective intervention shows that at-risk students are more successful when they are included in school-wide programs that emphasize meaningful, engaged learning, higher-order thinking skills, real-life problem solving, cooperative learning, and thematic or integrated instruction.[10] A school-wide program based on information literacy instruction emphasizes all these skills and instructional practices.

SUMMARY

Why is information literacy so important? It is important because we cannot possibly teach our students all they will need to know to survive and succeed. They must be able to learn new ideas and skills both independently and as members of a learning community, and use this information to solve problems, to make decisions, and to lead happy and productive lives. The crucial need to teach and foster information literacy skills is supported by national documents, standardized testing practices, and research on instructional goals for all students.

APPLYING THE STANDARDS

The following examples are based on actual assignments, curriculum information, and events that have taken place at an elementary school. The examples have been divided into the three categories identified in the AASL/AECT Standards, and the indicators that apply are marked in parentheses following the illustration of how the skill in that indicator was used. For example: "Before beginning work, the student made a list of what she knew and didn't know about the subject (1-1)." In this example, (1-1) denotes standard 1, indicator 1: The student who is information literate . . . recognizes the need for information.

Information Literacy Standards

Mrs. McKinney, fourth-grade teacher, has just assigned the following task to her students. They are to prepare a report on a particular state and identify certain items, for example, state flower, flag, governor, etc. They are to find out about the state's resources, tourist information, and population. They are then to produce a report on the state, an art project illustrating the state symbols, and a flyer promoting the state's "good" points, so that someone may want to visit.

Tamara sees this as a huge assignment and thinks for a while about where she wants to start. After pondering the assignment for some time, she decides first to make a list of what she already knows and what she doesn't know about her state (1-1). She also breaks the assignment into parts so that she can decide what she should tackle first, what she finds most difficult, and which part she will enjoy the most. Tamara then asks herself what she needs to find out (1-3) and marks by each area in which source she thinks she might find the information (1-4).

Tamara is lucky enough to have a computer at home, which she has learned how to use with help from her mom. She has games she plays on the computer, and, with her mother's guidance, has also used the Internet to find information. She decides to find some of the information she needs on the Web, but knows that for the more comprehensive parts of her assignment (1-2) she will have to use her school library's encyclopedias and books on the individual states, which she can find in the 900 section.

She develops her plan for gathering all the information she needs (1-5). When she looks on the Internet, she types in her state name and gets lots of hits. She must scroll through the many topics to find those she thinks might best suit her subject. Because there is so much "stuff," she narrows her search by typing her state's name and tourism; this is the part of the assignment for which she thinks the Internet is the best choice (1-4, 1-5). Her mom points out that Tamara must be careful what she selects because there are lots of advertisements for different locales, hotels, and events (2-1). The ads are placed there to sell products and may not necessarily contain true facts (2-2, 2-3). Tamara finds a site published by the chamber of commerce and feels that they probably have the most accurate information; she does find a lot of helpful information at this site (2-4).

After gathering information on state history, commerce, and occupations from the encyclopedias in the library; information on the state flag, tree, and flower from a book about her state; information on the governor and population statistics from the almanac; and information on tourism from the Web, Tamara is ready to wade through all her information. She must decide which information she can use, what facts address the original topic Mrs. McKinney assigned (3-1), and then organize the information into a report, a poster, and a tourist brochure (3-4).

She's seen tourist brochures before and decides to use her computer to produce one on her state (3-2). She must also look at the map of her state that she downloaded from the Internet and plot a travel route from her home state to the state she is studying. She must decide the best roads and highways to travel and identify which important tourist destinations to mark (3-3). Her poster is also going to be in "advertisement" form, similar to some of the posters she's seen around town that advertise plays and concerts (3-2, 3-4). She types her report on her computer, because she can type as fast as she can write, and besides, her word processing program has spell check!

Mrs. McKinney is very impressed with Tamara's finished project.

Independent Learning Standards

Three siblings who are very interested in animals attend Somewhere Elementary School. The two girls are in third and fourth grades, and their little brother is in first grade. They are constantly in the media center, checking out books on animals (4-1, 5-1). Somehow they rescue a flying squirrel and come into the media center again to look for information on how to care for the animal. After looking at all the information, as well as talking with a veterinarian, they discover that the animal is a sugar glider (5-2). After making this discovery, they look on the Internet and in encyclopedias for information concerning sugar gliders and their care (5-1). They gather their information and then plan to build a cage that has all the necessary "habitat" ingredients present for the sugar glider to survive. They also talk with the vet again to find out what to feed their pet (4-2). Their pet thrives. The oldest student decides to use her sugar glider as the basis for a book report she has to prepare. She organizes all the information she has gathered on her pet and creates a report, citing all the resources—books, encyclopedias, Internet, veterinarian—that she has found (4-2). For her presentation to the class, she has her grandfather bring in both the pet and the cage that she and her siblings have built for the animal (5-3). After preparing her report, the student discovers other facts about the sugar glider she didn't know before (6-2). She decides that she and her sister and brother need to redo the cage to make it more "user friendly" for their pet (6-1).

Social Responsibility Standards

Students in Mrs. Smith's fifth-grade class are studying a curriculum designed around certain character traits, such as responsibility, caring, respect, and honesty. Her curriculum is also multicultural and literature-based. The class decides to find out as much as possible about the places they visit through their studies. They want to explore the African country of Sierra Leone through the people's culture, lifestyles, and food. When they decide what information they need, they form three groups that will work together while gathering information (9-4). They plan to have a culminating presentation and celebration to share what they have learned with everyone in the fifth grade (9-1). They start by contacting people in the community to find out who may have family that came from this part of Africa. They discover that many of the area's families are descended from slaves who were brought to the United States from Sierra Leone. They make appointments to visit these residents and interview them (7-1). Meanwhile, other students are gathering information from various sources, including the Internet. They make sure that they site their sources (8-2), and take turns looking up information on the Internet (7-2). These students know that even though they have the right to use the Internet for their research (8-1), they must use it responsibly (8-3).

When they have gathered all the information, these students get together in their groups to organize the information and plan their presentation and celebration (9-1). They listen to each other and decide which information to include (9-2). One group arranges to have community members come in and discuss the problems that still exist for families whose ancestors came from Sierra Leone (9-3). Another group designs a PowerPoint presentation depicting some of the problems that still exist in Sierra Leone, then sponsors a debate during which class members discuss solutions to those problems (9-3). For their culminating celebration, a third group prepares a meal based on recipes that have been handed down in the families of community residents. They invite the members of the community that they interviewed to share their feast (9-1).

NOTES

1.   From *Information Power: Building Partnerships for Learning* by American Association of School Libraries and Association for Educational Communications and Technology. Copyright © 1998 American Library Association and Association for Educational Communications and Technology. Reprinted by permission of the American Library Association. For the past decade, *Information Power: Guidelines for School Library Media Programs* has been considered the guiding light and the handbook for library media specialists and for schools seeking to serve the information needs of all students. It states the mission of the library media program, then outlines ways it will be accomplished—specifying the changes that need to occur. The mission remains the same in the revised edition, *Information Power: Building Partnerships for Learning*.

2. One Hundred Third Congress of the United States of America, 1994, *GOALS 2000: Educate America Act*. URL: http://www.ed.gov/legislation/GOALS 2000/TheAct/. (Accessed November 8, 1999). As part of the official Web site for educational legislation, this Web page presents the table of contents of the act and provides links to each section. The section we have quoted is Sec. 102: National Education Goals.

3. One Hundred Third Congress of the United States of America, 1994, *National Education Goals*. URL: http://www.ed.gov/legislation/GOALS2000/TheAct/sec102.html. (Accessed November 8, 1999). The quote comes from the description of Goal 3, "Student Achievement and Citizenship."

4. Ibid., Goal 3, Objectives ii, iii, vi.

5. One Hundred Third Congress, GOALS 2000: Educate America Act, Goal 6, "Adult Literacy and Lifelong Learning."

6. Ibid.

7. Secretary's Commission on Achieving Necessary Skills, *What Work Requires of Schools: A SCANS Report for America 2000* (Washington, DC: U.S. Government Printing Office, 1991). This government document outlines the skills and abilities necessary for successful employment in today's workforce. The skills are divided into two categories: Foundation Skills and Competencies. The Foundation Skills include Basic Skills (reading, writing, arithmetic and mathematics, and speaking and listening), Thinking Skills (ability to learn, to reason, to think creatively, to make decisions, and to solve problems), and Personal Qualities (individual responsibility, self-esteem and self-management, sociability, and integrity). The Competencies include knowing how to use resources, interpersonal skills, information, systems, and technology. Ensuring that students acquire these three Foundation Skills and five Competencies is the purpose of the School-to-Work movement in schools nationwide. Students who are information literate will have a foundation of thinking skills and will be competent users of information and technology. This citation is related to the Thinking Skills.

8. Department of Evaluation and Research, *A Home Guide to Understanding MAT7* (Charleston, SC: Charleston County School District, 1998). This guide was developed by the Charleston County School District to help parents better understand the norm-referenced Metropolitan Achievement Tests, Seventh Edition, which is administered to students in Charleston County. The booklet was distributed in April 1998 to all CCSD schools in sufficient quantities for distribution to all parents. It has also been used in the Parent Teacher Student Association meetings and parenting sessions throughout the county. It explains what the MAT7 is, why it is given, and how parents can help their children do their best on the test. It includes sample questions from each subject area.

9. J. Hixson and M. B. Tinzmann, 1990, *Who Are the "At-Risk" Students of the 1990s?* URL: http://www.ncrel.org/sdrs/areas/rpl_esys/equity.htm. (Accessed August 27, 1999). This article is part of the North Central Regional Educational Laboratory's Web site and is ninth in a series about restructuring schools to support the belief that all students can learn. The authors describe the traditional approaches to identifying an at-risk student, then offer their theory that "at-riskness" is not determined by any one factor or circumstance, but may be affected by the organization of the school, the student's personal

or family characteristics or circumstances, the community surrounding the student and the school, and the relationship of all these to each other. The authors go on to explain why we need to focus on at-risk students, some barriers for them, and how to develop a thinking curriculum for all students. Thinking skills, problem solving, group participation, and the activities that promote them are stressed as critical for the success of at-risk students.

10.   Donna M. Ogle, *Critical Issue: Rethinking Learning for Students at Risk* (Brook, IL: The North Central Regional Educational Laboratory, 1997). URL: http://www.ncrel. org/sdrs/areas/issues/students/atrisk/at700.htm. (Accessed August 27, 1999). Pathway to School Improvement Internet Server: http://www.ncrel.org/sdrs/pathwayg.htm. Excerpted with permission. This article discusses the issue of at-risk students, who "often receive a watered-down curriculum that emphasizes the acquisition of basic academic skills," and suggests that "all students—especially those at risk—need to be engaged in interesting and challenging learning that goes beyond basic proficiencies." The site includes comments and audio files from experts in the field, and sections on goals to improve learning for at-risk students, action options, implementation pitfalls, and different points of view. The article supplies numerous links to related Web sites.

ADDITIONAL READINGS

Goals 2000

Goals 2000 Legislation and Related Items. 1998. URL: http://www.ed.gov/G2K/. Accessed August 27, 1999. As the title suggests, this site provides information about Goals 2000 with many links to sites concerning related items: academic standards, parent information, teacher connections, updates, etc.

The National Education Goals Panel. 1998. *National Education Goals: Building a Nation of Learners.* URL: http://www.negp.gov/WEBPG10.htm. Accessed August 27, 1999. This site provides links to each of the eight national education goals. Detailed descriptions of the objectives of the goals are given on the linked sites.

SCANS Report

SCANS/2000: The Workforce Skills Website. URL: http://www.scans.jhu.edu/workplace. html. Accessed November 9, 1999. This site provides an outline of the three Foundation Skills and the five Competencies necessary for graduates to earn a living and enjoy life.

Whetzel, Deborah. *The Secretary of Labor's Commission on Achieving Necessary Skills.* (ED 339 749). This ERIC Digest document explains the necessity of workplace skills, states the skills, and describes the commission's process of identifying and defining the skills and identifying levels of skill difficulty.

Standardized Tests

Adcock, Deborah. *Test Ready Language Arts.* North Billerica, MA: Curriculum Associates, 1996. This practice booklet includes sample test questions and test-taking tips. Questions on resources are incorporated into each section of the practice test.

Balow, Irving H. *MAT7 Instructional Objectives: Grades K–12.* San Antonio, TX: The Psychological Corporation, 1993. This guide was designed to explain the scope and sequence of MAT7 questions and the cognitive abilities required for each grade level. According to the document, Thinking Skills questions are asked in the Reading Comprehension, Mathematics, Language, Science, and Social Studies tests. Thinking Skills involve analyzing, synthesizing, evaluating, and extrapolating information. Research Skills questions are found in the Mathematics, Language, Science, and Social Studies tests as well. They measure students' ability to locate and use information from a variety of sources. All these are information literacy skills.

South Carolina Department of Education. 1998. *Sample Test Questions.* URL: http://www.state.sc.us/sde/test123/sample.htm. Accessed November 8, 1999. South Carolina has developed a new state test, the Palmetto Achievement Challenge Test, or PACT, to take the place of one that is over twenty years old. This site offers sample mini-tests or sample test questions for different grade levels. Another link (http://www.state.sc.us/sde/test123/compques.htm) compares questions from the old test to sample questions from the new. Many of the new questions ask about processes and procedures and require written answers.

At-Risk Students

Costello, Mary Ann. 1996. *Providing Effective Schooling for Students at Risk.* URL: http://www.ncrel.org/sdrs/areas/issues/students/atrisk/at600.htm. Accessed November 8, 1999. A part of the North Central Regional Educational Laboratory's (NCREL) Web site, this critical-issue site focuses on the goals and action options of effective at-risk programs. It also discusses implementation pitfalls and offers some different viewpoints. Links throughout provide further explanations of the terms and topics discussed. It concludes with links to illustrative-case schools and additional contacts.

Donnelly, Margarita. *At-Risk Students.* Eugene, OR: ERIC Clearinghouse on Educational Management, 1987. ED 292 172. URL: http://ed.gov/databases/ERIC_Digests/ed292172.html. Accessed November 8, 1999. This ERIC Digest article answers questions about the characteristics of at-risk students, when and how they can be identified, what kinds of programs are effective, and how the current push for excellence affects at-risk students.

Ogle, Donna M. 1997. *Meaningful, Engaged Learning.* URL: http://www.ncrel.org/sdrs/engaged.htm. Accessed November 8, 1999. This link from the *Rethinking Learning for Students at Risk* site tells just what meaningful, engaged learning is. It defines tasks and assessments of engaged learning, discusses grouping and instructional models for engaged learning, and highlights the roles of teacher and student.

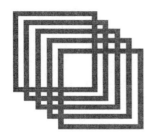

Chapter **3**

How Information Literacy Relates to National Curriculum Standards

*A teacher affects eternity; he can
never tell where his influence stops.*
—Henry Brooks Adams

Although it is true that we can't tell where a teacher's influence stops, we do know that it starts in the classroom and within the curriculum. A teacher's knowledge and presentation of subject-area content has a great influence on how much information students absorb. The real measure of lasting influence, however, is how valuable this information is years after the test, the paper, or the oral report. If the information learned includes concepts, skills, or attitudes that will benefit students for the rest of their lives, the teacher's influence truly never stops.

The national curriculum guidelines and standards recognize the importance of learning concepts, skills, and attitudes over memorizing individual facts. The mathematics standards emphasize mathematics as problem solving and reasoning, so that students draw logical conclusions and believe that mathematics makes sense (see appendix A). The science standards stress scientific inquiry and technological design so that students learn to identify a problem, and propose, implement, and evaluate a solution (see appendix B). National history standards call for the analysis of primary documents and data (see appendix C), and the language arts standards highlight independent learning and communication skills (see appendix D). Even the fine arts standards stress the importance of students' critical- and creative-thinking skills when solving problems in movement and when distinguishing among design elements to select the most appropriate medium for the message (see appendix E). These information literacy skills, proposed by all the national curriculum standards, will serve students for the rest of their lives, not just until the end of the grading period.

Another common idea proposed by the national standards for math, science, social studies, language arts, and fine arts is the need for reform—the need to change the way we teach. The recommended changes are the same as those proposed for information literacy instruction (as outlined in chapter 5): more hands-on activities, more resource-based learning, more problem solving, and less lecture and memorization.[1]

An analysis of the different national curriculum guidelines shows they are related to the information literacy standards in one of three ways: 1) they resemble specific information literacy standards, 2) students will need information literacy skills to master them, or 3) they will be achieved by the same instructional methods used for fostering information literacy. These relationships are discussed in this chapter and also are depicted in charts (appendixes A, B, C, D, and E) in an attempt to convince classroom teachers that information literacy instruction is not an added responsibility, but is naturally a part of everyday instruction. In the charts, the subject-area standards have been placed on the left to emphasize their importance and the corresponding information literacy standards on the right to illustrate their supporting characteristics. This same arrangement is recommended when aligning information literacy standards with state or district frameworks or guidelines.

MATHEMATICS

The math standards selected for evaluation are offered by the National Council of Teachers of Mathematics (NCTM). The specific standards used in the chart are written for kindergarten through fourth grade and are statements about what is valued in mathematics curricula; they define what it means to be mathematically literate. The NCTM formally adopted these standards "to ensure quality, to indicate goals, and to promote change."[2]

The relationships of the math standards to the information literacy standards follow the three patterns specified above—similar, necessary for mastery, or achieved by the same methods. The broad mathematical literacy goals supported by the math standards state that all students 1) learn to value mathematics, 2) become confident in their ability to do mathematics, 3) become mathematical problem solvers, 4) learn to communicate mathematically, and 5) learn to reason mathematically.[3] These mathematical literacy goals echo the information literacy standards of independent learning, applying information in critical thinking and problem solving, and communicating information effectively. The increased use of calculators and computers requires the responsible use of information technology, another information literacy standard. Finally, the math goals will be achieved by the same teaching methods and practices that foster information literacy instruction: more genuine problem-solving activities, more emphasis on understanding concepts and processes, more integration with other subjects, more use of information resources, more cooperative work, and less rote memorization and reliance on worksheets with isolated math computations.

According to the first standard, Mathematics as Problem Solving, the study of mathematics should emphasize problem solving so that students can investigate everyday problems and identify and use strategies to solve them, and by doing so, gain confidence in using mathematics meaningfully. These goals relate directly to the information literacy objectives of formulating questions, applying information in critical thinking and problem solving, and devising strategies for improving learning.

Mathematics as Communication, another standard, stresses the importance of providing students opportunities to reflect upon and discuss mathematical ideas, language, and symbols and relate these to their everyday lives. Corresponding information literacy objectives include seeking information related to personal interests, communicating information, and integrating new information into one's own knowledge.

Standard 3, Mathematics as Reasoning, states that the study of mathematics should emphasize reasoning so that students can draw logical conclusions about mathematics and can justify their answers and how they arrived at them. These math objectives correspond most closely to the information literacy goals of having students evaluate their information and their information-seeking processes, and use this information to solve problems.

Even the standards for specific mathematical concepts such as estimation, numeration, whole-number operations and computations, geometry, measurement, statistics, fractions, and patterns are supported by information literacy objectives. Many of these require students to understand information presented in a variety of ways and to present and communicate it in appropriate formats. Others require students to organize information for practical purposes. All of them require students to use information in critical thinking and problem solving.

In appendix A, the K–4 math standards are listed on the left and the corresponding information literacy standards and indicators are listed on the right. The number following the information literacy standard denotes the number of that particular standard and indicator, for example, 1.0 indicates standard 1; 1.3 is standard 1, indicator 3.

SCIENCE

The National Science Education Standards were developed by the National Research Council's National Committee on Science Education Standards and Assessment (NCSESA) and are available on the Internet and in print. This document contains not only science content standards but also science system standards, science program standards, science teaching and professional development standards, and science assessment standards.[4] When these are compared to the information literacy standards, the science program standards and the science teaching standards are just as valuable as the science content standards. They both stress the same instructional methods that are necessary for information literacy instruction. Program standard B states that the study of science should be developmentally appropriate, interesting, and relevant to students' lives; should emphasize student understanding through inquiry; and should be connected to other school subjects. These specifications define an integrated, authentic, resource-based, problem-solving curriculum that fosters the development of information literacy skills in students. The teaching standards list the responsibilities, actions, and attitudes of teachers that support the program standards. As in the math curriculum reform and information literacy reform, the science teaching standards place more emphasis on students' understanding and use of knowledge, on ideas and thinking processes, on discussion and debate, on active learning, on students' individuality, and on cooperative learning. Less emphasis is placed on requiring students to learn and recite facts, on lecturing, on treating students equally, and on supporting competition between students (National Science Education Standards, chapter 3, "Changing Emphases for Teaching").

The National Science Education Content Standards are divided into seven sections: Science as Inquiry, Physical Science, Life Science, Earth and Space Science, Science and Technology, Science in Personal and Social Perspectives, and the History and Nature of Science. As illustrated in appendix B, the sections most directly related to information literacy objectives are Science as Inquiry, Science and Technology, Science in Personal and Social Perspectives, and the History and Nature of Science. However, the others do have some correlation and, as stated previously, should be taught and learned by the same instructional methods necessary for information literacy instruction.

The National Science content standard A, Science as Inquiry, states that all students should be able to conduct scientific inquiry. This includes asking questions about things or events in the natural world, using tools to gather data, using data to give reasonable answers to the questions, and communicating both the procedures and the results. The information literacy standards also state that students should be able to formulate questions, search for information, use information technology responsibly, evaluate information, apply it in critical thinking and problem solving, and share this knowledge with others.

The science standards stress that students understand some important concepts of scientific inquiry as well as the steps involved. One concept is that "scientific investigations involve asking and answering a question and comparing the answer with what scientists already know about the world" (content standard A). Information literacy also involves asking questions, and analyzing and evaluating the answers. Another scientific inquiry concept is that "scientists use different kinds of investigations depending on the questions they are trying to answer" (content standard A). Investigations can consist of describing things, classifying them, or performing experiments on them. Similar information literacy concepts demand that information-literate students formulate questions based on needs, use information technology responsibly, and organize information for practical applications. Finally, scientific inquiry requires that "scientists make the results of their investigations public; they describe the investigations in ways that enable others to repeat the investigations" (content standard A). The information literacy standard concerning social responsibility also requires that students "share their knowledge with others and collaborate with others to identify problems and to seek and evaluate their solutions."

Science Content Standards stress the development of an understanding of the history and nature of science (content standard G) and the use of "science in personal and social perspectives" (content standard F). In understanding the history of science and the contributions made by various men and women, students are developing the socially responsible attitudes of respect and appreciation for others' ideas. Seeing science in a personal and social perspective requires students to be independent learners as well as group participants.

The correlation between the National Science Education Content Standards and the Information Literacy Standards for Student Learning is depicted graphically in appendix B.

SOCIAL STUDIES

The National Standards for Grades K–4 History were published by the National Center for History in the Schools in 1995.[5] The standards are divided into two parts: historical thinking skills and historical understandings. Historical thinking skills "enable children to differentiate past, present, and future time; raise questions; seek and evaluate evidence; compare and analyze historical stories, illustrations, and records from the past; interpret the historical record; and construct historical narratives of their own."[6] These mimic the thinking skills promoted by the information literacy standards: formulating questions, accessing and evaluating information, using information in critical thinking, understanding information in different formats, and creating information products in appropriate formats.

For the elementary level, the historical understandings standards emphasize family life, communities, state history, democratic values, immigrations and migrations, folklore, other cultures, inventors and inventions, and the effects of major discoveries in technology, transportation, and communication (chapter 3). These standards may appear as strictly subject-area curriculum objectives;

however, the demonstrable objectives are closely related to information literacy skills and abilities.

National history standard 1 states "Students should understand family life now and in the recent past and family life in various places long ago." The objectives and activities listed in this standard require many information literacy skills. Beginning with their own families, students interview older relatives or look at documents to trace their roots for two generations. Using this information, they then create a family tree and a timeline of important events. They look at old photographs and records and draw conclusions about family life long ago and the roles various family members played. To accomplish these tasks, students must be able to identify a variety of potential sources of information, derive meaning from information presented creatively in a variety of formats, think critically, ask questions, and organize information.

Standard 1 also states that students should demonstrate understanding of the differences in groups of people. When students examine the beliefs of different cultures and then compare the dreams and ideals of various groups, they are distinguishing among fact, point of view, and opinion, and are thinking critically about the differences in racial or ethnic groups. Identifying a variety of information sources, understanding information presented in a variety of formats, thinking critically, formulating questions, organizing information, and distinguishing among fact, point of view, and opinion are all information literacy skills that either will be mastered along with the history objectives or must be mastered to accomplish the history objectives.

The same premise is true for the relationship between information literacy and the rest of the history standards. Standard 2 states, "Students should understand the history of their local community and how communities in North America varied long ago." Students study the history of their local communities by using population data and historical maps, which requires understanding information in a variety of formats.

Standard 3 focuses on state history: "Students should understand the people, events, problems, and ideas that were significant in creating the history of their state." The objectives for this standard require students to examine artifacts and research legends to learn about the original inhabitants of the state in which they reside. These activities are related to the information literacy skills of accessing and understanding information presented in many formats. To compare and contrast the difference between Native American life today and 100 years ago, students must be able to think critically about the information they have gathered. Students are accessing information, organizing it, applying it to critical thinking, and creating information products when they gather and analyze data for the reasons the settlers came, create timelines showing early explorations and settlements, use visual data to determine ways the settlers adapted to and changed the environment, analyze interactions between the native peoples of the state and the first settlers, and construct a historical narrative about daily life in the first settlements. In addition to learning about the native peoples and the early settlers of their state, students research the other groups that came to their area—what they were like, the reasons they came, the adjustments they made, and the changes they brought about. Researching these groups includes reading fiction and non-fiction accounts, listening to speakers, viewing photographs and pictures, examining newspapers and magazine accounts, and looking at census data to gain an understanding of the different groups, their contributions, their problems, and their interactions with each other. Many of these activities require or foster information literacy skills.

Standard 4 states, "Students should understand how democratic values came to be and how they have been exemplified by people, events, and symbols." Students' understanding should include knowledge about the fight for independence from England, the principles of democracy set forth in the Declaration of Independence and the Constitution, the struggles of individuals and groups to "achieve the liberties and equality promised in democracy" (standard 4A), and the contributions of both historic figures and ordinary citizens in the fight for democracy. It also should include knowledge about the historical events that contributed to democracy, the holidays that celebrate it, and the national symbols "through which American values and principles are expressed" (standard 4E). Understanding these values requires students to compare and analyze the people, events, and symbols that developed and now depict democracy; it requires them to use information to think critically. In addition to requiring an information literacy skill, the teaching of this standard fosters still others—respecting others' ideas and backgrounds and acknowledging their contributions, sharing knowledge and information with others, and respecting the principles of intellectual freedom.

Migration and immigration are the focus of standard 5, which reads, "Students should understand the causes and nature of various movements of large groups of people into and within the U.S. now and long ago." An emphasis on using primary documents, charts, and maps highlights again the need for information literacy skills such as developing successful strategies for locating information and deriving meaning from information presented in a variety of formats.

Developing an awareness of the nation's cultural heritage is the goal of standard 6: "Students should understand folklore and other cultural contributions from various regions of the U.S. and how they help to form a national heritage." Drawing again from information in a variety of formats (stories, legends, ballads, games, tall tales, art, crafts, music, and language), students examine the cultures of different peoples and describe their influences on the nation. As with standard 4, this standard not only requires the information literacy research, thinking, and communication skills but also fosters the information literacy concepts of respecting others' ideas and contributions and of respecting intellectual freedom.

Standard 7 says "Students should understand selected attributes and historical developments of societies in such places as Africa, the Americas, Asia, and Europe." For elementary students, the study of other countries focuses on the geography, communities, family life, customs, and culture of the continent. They analyze the art, music, dance, folktales, legends, myths, customs, and geography of a region to describe the daily life of the people and compare it to their own. In addition to other information literacy skills already mentioned, students learn to respect others' ideas and backgrounds.

The last standard emphasizes the major effects scientific developments in technology, transportation, and communication have had on the world and its communities. In this unit, students research famous inventors and their inventions, compare the behaviors of hunters and gatherers to those of farmers, illustrate the development of the wheel and its early uses, create timelines of transportation developments, and explain the significance of the printing press and the computer and their impact on the communication of ideas. This national history standard, like the others, requires information literacy skills and abilities and fosters their acquisition. The relationship of the information literacy standards to the National Standards for Grades K–4 History is depicted in a chart in appendix C.

ENGLISH LANGUAGE ARTS

The International Reading Association (IRA) and the National Council of Teachers of English (NCTE) cooperatively produced a set of national standards for English Language Arts in 1996.[7] The standards are published as a list of twelve skills and activities that literate students are capable of performing. The two associations stress the assumption that all students will have access to all the resources that are necessary to develop these abilities. They also emphasize that the standards should be considered as guidelines for creative and innovative curriculum development, not as prescriptions for specific instructional practices.

The English Language Arts (ELA) standards and Information Literacy Standards for Student Learning are closely related. Many of the ELA standards mirror information literacy standards. Others require the skills or attitudes fostered by information literacy instruction. For example, the ELA standards call for students to read a wide range of print and nonprint texts to learn about themselves and other people, and to read a wide range of literature to learn about human experiences. They are to read for knowledge and enjoyment and are expected to comprehend, interpret, and evaluate what they read. These guidelines correspond to the information literacy skills of seeking information from various sources for academic and personal reasons, deriving meaning from information presented in a variety of formats, and applying information in critical thinking.

The ELA standards expect students to speak and write appropriately, their messages adjusted to the audience and to the purpose of the communication. These goals are accomplished by fostering information literacy skills that enable students to communicate information and ideas in appropriate formats and to create information products in a variety of formats. ELA standards require students to "create, critique, and discuss print and nonprint texts" (ELA standard 6). Information literacy instruction ensures the ability to do this by teaching students to create information products in many different forms and to think critically about information presented in different formats. Information literacy instruction also encourages students to share and discuss their knowledge with others.

Research skills figure prominently in the ELA and the information literacy standards. Both expect students to ask appropriate questions, identify and evaluate suitable resources, and communicate their findings. Both expect students to do these things using a variety of technologies. Respect for others' ideas and culture is another common objective. The information literacy standards that pertain to social responsibility emphasize respect for others' ideas and backgrounds and acknowledgment of their contributions. The ELA standards promote this by encouraging students to look at language use, patterns, and dialects across cultures, ethnic groups, geographic regions, and social roles.

The links between the ELA standards and the AASL/AECT Information Literacy Standards for Student Learning are illustrated in a chart in appendix D. The curriculum standards are listed on the left side of the chart and the corresponding information literacy skills are on the right. The numbers following each information literacy skill denote the specific standard and indicator listed.

FINE ARTS

Fine Arts instruction is no longer considered a frill or an extra in our nation's schools. The Goals 2000: Educate America Act outlines national goals for arts education. The National Standards for Arts Education were developed to assist in achieving these fine arts goals for students.[8] The arts standards for dance, music, theater, and visual arts relate most directly to the information literacy standards of deriving meaning from information presented in a variety of formats, applying information in critical thinking, producing and communicating information and ideas in appropriate formats, appreciating and enjoying creative expressions of information, and developing creative products in a variety of formats. What are, perhaps, more revealing than the standards themselves are the explanations of high-quality arts education and the discussions about how it prepares students to live and work in an uncertain world. As the standards reflect, arts education for today's students provides more and demands more than just exposure to music, dance, drama, and visual arts. High-quality arts education fosters the same thinking skills that information literacy instruction fosters, and requires the same educational reforms as the math, science, history, and English language arts curricula.

Dr. Elliot Eisner, a professor of education and art at Stanford University, offers eight thinking skills that a high-quality arts education program teaches exceptionally well:

- The perception of relationships—the arts help students recognize that nothing stands alone.

- Attention to nuance—the arts teach students that small differences can have large effects.

- The arts foster an awareness that problems can have multiple solutions and questions multiple answers—that good things can be done in different ways.

- Work in the arts develops the ability to shift aims in process—to recognize and pursue goals that were not conceptualized at the outset.

- The arts foster the ability to make decisions in the absence of rule—for example, to decide when work is completed.

- The arts call upon imagination as a source of content—the ability to visualize situations and consider in the mind's eye the rightness of planned action. The cultivation of imagination . . . ought to be at the center of our educational aims.

- The arts develop the student's ability to operate within the constraints of a medium. . . . Giving young people a chance to address the constraints of a medium helps them invent ways to exploit constraints productively.

- The arts develop the ability to frame the world from an aesthetic perspective.[9]

Eisner also states that arts education not only prepares students for an uncertain future by encouraging them to "think beyond boundaries" but also enriches their lives and expands what they can know, what they can imagine, and what they can feel. "A school's mission is wider than learning how to make a living. It is a place where students can learn how to make a life. . . . The arts are among the important ways we can remake ourselves" (Eisner, 5). The ultimate goal of information literacy instruction is also to prepare students for an uncertain future and to empower them to enrich their lives by becoming lifelong learners. Therefore, high-quality arts education and information literacy instruction go hand in hand.

The chart in appendix E shows the relationship between the fine arts standards for dance, music, theater, and visual arts and the Information Literacy Standards for Student Learning. The number following each information literacy objective denotes the specific standard and indicator listed. For example, 3.0 indicates standard 3; 3.3 stands for standard 3, indicator 3.

SUMMARY

The national curriculum guidelines and standards recognize the importance of learning the concepts, skills, and attitudes of information literacy. The mathematics standards emphasize mathematics as problem solving and reasoning. The science standards stress scientific inquiry and technological design. National history standards call for the analysis of primary documents and data, and the language arts standards highlight independent learning and communication skills. Even the fine arts standards stress applying critical- and creative-thinking skills. These information literacy skills, proposed by all the national curriculum standards, will serve students throughout their lives.

NOTES

1.   Reprinted with permission from *Curriculum and Evaluation Standards for School Mathematics*, copyright © 1989 by the National Council of Teachers of Mathematics. All rights reserved. Also found on the Internet at URL: http://www.enc.org/reform/journals/ enc2280/nf_280dtoc1.htm, this document not only gives national standards for mathematics instruction but also tells why new standards and goals are needed and why change is needed to achieve them. In the section "The Need for Change," the document states, "A long-standing preoccupation with computation and other traditional skills has dominated both what mathematics is taught and the way mathematics is taught. . . . As a result, the present K–4 curriculum is narrow in scope; fails to foster mathematical insight, reasoning, and problem solving; and emphasizes rote activities. Even more significant is that children begin to lose their belief that learning mathematics is a sense-making experience. They become passive receivers of rules and procedures rather than active participants in creating knowledge."

2.   Ibid. The document gives Curriculum Standards for grades K–4, 5–8, and 9–12, Evaluation Standards, and the "Next Steps" in changing school mathematics. We recommend that all library media specialists and math teachers study the introduction as well as the curriculum standards. The introduction provides valuable insight into the goals of mathematics education for an information society and the changing emphases of mathematics instruction. The curriculum standards for each level are organized by concepts such as "Mathematics as Problem Solving," "Mathematics as Communication," "Mathematics as Reasoning," etc. Each standard specifies indicators of desirable student awareness or performance within that concept.

3.   Ibid.

4.   Reprinted with permission from *National Science Education Standards*. Copyright © 1995 by the National Academy of Sciences. Courtesy of the National Academy Press, Washington, DC. URL: http://www.nap.edu/readingroom/books/nses/html/index.html. (Accessed November 8, 1999). This document includes six Science Teaching Standards and the changing emphases for teaching, four Standards for Professional Development for Teachers of Science and the changing emphases for professional development, five Assessment Standards and their changing emphases, Science Content Standards for

grades K–4, 5–8, and 9–12, six Science Education Program Standards, and seven Science Education System Standards. Examples and References for Further Reading are given for each.

5.   National Center for History in the Schools, *National Standards for Grades K–4 History* (Los Angeles: National Center for History in the Schools, 1995). By permission of the National Center for History in the Schools at UCLA. This document discusses why educated citizens need to study history, how the standards were developed, and what policies are necessary for successful implementation. The policies include "ensuring equity for all students," "providing adequate instructional time for history," and "linking history to other related studies in an integrated or interdisciplinary curriculum." While one section defines the difference between historical thinking and historical understandings, another stresses the integration of the two. The standards presented in chapter 3 represent a blending of both thinking skills and understanding; they consist of eight standards organized into four distinct topics. The electronic version can be found on the Internet at http://www.sscnet.ucla.edu/nchs/usk4-toc.htm. (Accessed November 8, 1999).

6.   Ibid. Chapter 1: "Developing Standards in History for Students in Grades K–4."

7.   *Standards for the English Language Arts* by the International Reading Association and National Council of Teachers of English. Copyright 1996 by the International Reading Association and the National Council of Teachers of English. Reprinted with permission. A copy of the twelve standards can be found on the Internet at http://www.didaxinc.com/standards/langstandards.html. These standards represent the language skills all students need to "pursue life's goals and to participate fully as informed, productive members of society." The developers emphasize that the skills are "not distinct and separate; they are, in fact, interrelated and should be considered as a whole."

8.   Excerpted from *National Standards for Arts Education*, published by Music Educators National Conference (MENC). Copyright © 1994 by MENC. Reproduced with permission. The complete National Arts Standards and additional materials relating to the Standards are available from MENC—The National Association for Music Education, 1806 Robert Fulton Drive, Reston, VA 20191 (telephone 800-336-3768). The National Standards for Arts Education outline "what every young American should know and be able to do in the arts." These standards are divided into the four disciplines of dance, music, theater, and visual arts. The disciplines are further subdivided into grade-level groups. Each level builds on the previous one and students are expected to steadily progress in both skills and understanding of the arts. The online version of the standards can be found at http://www.mcrel.org/standards-benchmarks/standardslib/art.html (Kendall, John S. and Marzano, Robert J. [1997]. *Content Knowledge: A Compendium of Standards and Benchmarks for K–12 Education*, 2nd ed. Aurora, CO: McREL. Used by permission of McREL).

9.   Elliot Eisner, "Educating for Tomorrow's Jobs and Life Skills," *Arts Education for Life and Work* (November 1997): 4–5. Reprinted by permission. This article details thinking skills that can be illustrated and taught through arts education, and provides a rationale for the intrinsic value of arts education. Other articles in the insert are "Arts Education for a Changing World"; "The Arts: Dynamic Partner in Building Strong Schools"; "What Kinds of Jobs? What Kinds of Skills?"; "What's Standard About Arts

Education?"; "What Are They Saying About Arts Education and Effective School Reform?"; "The Future of Imagination"; "Arts Education for a Lifetime of Wonder"; and "Learning About Art from a Global Perspective."

ADDITIONAL READINGS

Annenberg/CPB Projects. 1998. *The Guide to Math and Science Reform*. URL: http://www. learner.org/theguide/. Accessed November 8, 1999. This interesting and informative site provides a database of math and science reform initiatives and organizations. Searches can be defined by school level, content focus, reform focus, location, technologies, and type of initiative and funding.

Consortium of National Arts Education Associations. 1994. *National Standards for Arts Education*. URL: http://artsedge.kennedy-center.org/cs/design/standards/index.html. Accessed November 8, 1999. This online version of the arts standards document includes an introduction that highlights the benefits of an arts education, explores the importance of standards in arts education, and details the standards themselves.

Hill, Charles. 1998. *Developing Educational Standards*: *Overview*. URL: http://putwest. boces.org/standards.html. Accessed November 8, 1999. Sponsored by Putnam Valley Central Schools, this site is an annotated index of educational standards. The standards may by accessed by subject area or by organization. There are also links to U.S. government sites and standards from other nations and focus groups.

Holland Public Schools. 1992. *State and National Curriculum Standards*. URL: http://www.macatawa.org/~paws/hps/curric.standards.html. Accessed November 8, 1999. Another Web site with links to national standards for all subjects.

Mid-Continent Regional Educational Laboratory. 1996. *Mathematics Standards*. URL: http://www.mcrel.org/standards-benchmarks/standardslib/math.html. Accessed November 8, 1999. This McREL site lists nine general standards for mathematics for all ages. References to comparable national and state guidelines are given for each standard. The site also contains links to Math Internet Connections for lesson plans, etc.

Mid-Continent Regional Educational Laboratory. 1996. *Science Standards*. URL: http://www.mcrel.org/standards-benchmarks/standardslib/science.html. Accessed November 8, 1999. There are sixteen general science standards listed on this page, which is similar to the McRel Math Standards Web page. Each standard is documented with state and national guidelines. The site provides valuable links to lesson plans and other Internet connections.

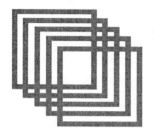

Chapter 4

Essential Components of Information Literacy

Knowledge is of two kinds.
We know a subject ourselves or we know
where we can find information upon it.

—Samuel Johnson

Finding information "upon" or about a subject is one of the essential components of information literacy. The ability to find or to access information is a major characteristic of an information-literate person. So are the abilities to evaluate and use the newfound information. Although these are not the only characteristics of an information-literate person, they form the foundation upon which the other skills rest. Information-literate people also should be able to learn independently, work effectively in groups, use information technology responsibly, respect the principles of intellectual freedom, and observe copyright laws. However, information-seeking, evaluating, and synthesizing skills are crucial to deriving meaning from information. As Samuel Johnson said, they are one kind of knowledge.

THE RESEARCH PROCESS

Studies have shown that people who successfully find information on a subject follow a certain path or take specific steps during their searches. This path is known as the *research process*. The process includes basic activities such as thinking about the problem, question, or topic, identifying possible sources of information, searching for (accessing) information in those resources, organizing the information for better understanding, and sharing this information with others. Sometimes the path will be straightforward from beginning to end, but more often it will circle back and around as the searcher rethinks a question, identifies more resources, or revises a search strategy. Whether linear or circular, the path the research process follows depends on the searcher, the specific question, problem, or topic, and the availability of resources.

The Models

The research process can be taught, and *must* be taught if students are to become information literate. There are several research process models, developed by educators, that describe the steps and outline the path an information-literate person follows when seeking information. Those considered for this chapter are Information Problem-Solving: The Big Six Skills™ Approach to Library and Information Skills Instruction developed by Michael B. Eisenberg and Robert E. Berkowitz[1]; InfoZone, from the Assiniboine South School Division of Winnipeg, Canada[2]; Pathways to Knowledge: Follett's Information Skills Model, by Marjorie Pappas and Ann Tepe[3]; Organized Investigator (Circular Model), created by David Loertscher[4] and presented on the California Technology Assistance Program, Region VII's Web site; The Research Cycle Revisited, created by Jamieson McKenzie[5]; and Information Literacy: Dan's Generic Model, developed by Daniel Barron.[6]

All these models incorporate the basic activities of identifying, accessing, evaluating, and using information, but differ slightly in their approaches to pre- and post-search activities. Each model is discussed specifically in the notes at the end of this chapter. It is recommended that teachers and library media specialists adopt an appropriate research process school-wide or grade-wide, discuss and model this process with students, and implement it through assignments and activities. The adopted research process does not have to be one of the above-mentioned models, nor does it have to be any of the other published models not mentioned. A generic model, which is developed by the teachers and library media specialists of each school and which incorporates the most appropriate components of each, will achieve the same results. More significant than the particular process chosen is the consistency in teaching and modeling whichever process is adopted.

The Process

Appreciating and Enjoying Information

This step is acknowledged in the Pathways to Knowledge model only, but it may well be the phase that creates lifelong learners, the primary goal of information literacy instruction. According to Pappas and Tepe, students appreciate and enjoy information by viewing, listening, and reading. Teachers and library media specialists encourage these activities by providing stimulating, information-rich environments and allowing students ample opportunities to explore and appreciate them. Teachers and library media specialists also promote this attitude by modeling a delight in discovery and expressing their own joy in learning and knowing.

> *Just what is an information-rich environment? One that is filled with books, learning centers, jars with bugs, posters with thought-provoking sayings, shells, rocks, aquariums. Students can listen to favorite tapes at listening centers, hear stories of their choice, or watch a favorite ETV (educational television) show that highlights a book just read by the class. Most of us already provide classrooms such as these for our students. But the process goes one step further—with teachers and library media specialists showing their own interests in new things. For instance, when a student asks a question, take that lead and have the class find the answer. While Mrs. Henley was reading a book about doves to her classes, several students asked how homing pigeons found their way. She told them she didn't know, but invited those who would like to find out back to the media center to help discover the answer.*

Wondering

This term is taken from the InfoZone model. Specifically, it means asking questions about something or defining the need for information. The Big6 Skills™ Approach calls this step a "task definition" in which students consider an information problem or question and decide on the information needed to solve the problem or answer the question. The first of the Big6™ research guidelines for younger students asks, "What is my question? Is it a good question?"

The Pathways to Knowledge model uses the term "questions," which refers to a student's desire to learn more for fun or for a specific purpose. The Organized Investigator, a circular model, says the researcher "questions and wonders," "formulates and shapes an inquiry," and is inquisitive. In this section of the process, the researcher brainstorms to formulate questions and narrow or broaden the topic.

The Research Cycle also calls this phase "questioning" and focuses on the framing of "essential questions." According to McKenzie, essential questions possess the following main attributes: They require that students use the thinking skills at the top of Bloom's Taxonomy and call for students to evaluate, synthesize, or analyze information. Next, essential questions mirror situations concerning real-life problem solving or decision making; they also have the ability to spark students' curiosity or sense of wonder. Most important, the "answers to essential questions cannot be found. They must be invented." Students must create insight and "construct their own answers" to essential questions. During the questioning phase, students also identify smaller or subsidiary questions that will help them answer their larger questions. The focus on essential questions raises the research process from a mere topical search to an exciting quest for meaning and answers.

Dan's Generic Model approach lists "formulating a question" as the first step in the research process. The question may originate with the teacher or the student. Student-generated questions often are more successful because the search becomes personalized. All students are curious. All wonder about something. By allowing students to research topics of personal interest, teachers and library media specialists harness this curiosity, give it direction, and use it to teach information literacy skills.

> *A class of first-graders has been learning about dinosaurs. They have looked at pictures, read some books, and drawn pictures of dinosaurs. They want to know more and when the teacher asks them what they want to do next, they tell her they want to do research! The delighted teacher sits down with the class, and the students ask several questions, which the teacher writes down. These questions range from what did dinosaurs eat to why did they die. The teacher then tells the students to think hard about what they want to know the most and then they will write down five questions to answer. She decides to schedule a field trip to the museum, which has an exhibit of dinosaurs visiting this month. There, the children can interview an expert on dinosaurs. The next day, the students discuss their questions again; they come up with the following five:*
>
> 1.   *What was the earth like when dinosaurs were alive?*
> 2.   *Which dinosaurs were the largest? Which dinosaurs were the smallest?*
> 3.   *What did dinosaurs eat?*
> 4.   *How long did dinosaurs live?*
> 5.   *What happened to the dinosaurs?*

Background Building

The Pathways to Knowledge model inserts another step, "presearch," before the "information seeking" phase of the research process. During presearch, the information-literate person builds background knowledge by browsing general sources. Pathways considers the presearch step important and necessary for building an overview of the topic. During this stage, students relate what they want to know to what they already know and gather enough broad information on a chosen topic to continue the search intelligently.

> *The first-grade class performed some presearch steps in learning about dinosaurs. They explored nonfiction books about dinosaurs, looked at different pictures of dinosaurs, and drew and colored pictures of various dinosaurs. They also learned some of the names of the different species as well as certain facts, like which dinosaurs were largest, which were smallest, etc.*

Seeking Information

The processes and skills used in the information-seeking stage are primarily traditional library research skills. The Big6 Skills™ Approach has two stages— "information seeking strategies" and "location and access"—that focus on seeking information. In these stages, students identify and locate a variety of resources, select the best, and then access the information in them by using a table of contents, an index, Boolean searching, etc. Younger students are encouraged to ask, "How can I get my information?" and "Where can I find this information?" InfoZone calls the process "seeking," but the concept is the same—locating and accessing a variety of resources. InfoZone stresses seeking multiple sources to aid in understanding and choosing the right keywords to facilitate seeking.

When students "search" (Pathways to Knowledge terminology), they formulate specific questions about a topic and map a search strategy, considering both information providers and resources before searching for relevant material. In The Research Cycle, "planning" comes before "gathering." Students identify sources likely to increase their knowledge of a subject, then gather and store information for later use. They are encouraged to keep an open mind when hunting for information and to review it frequently; possibly they will revise their questions, strategies, and resources.

The Organized Investigator "finds and sorts" information while "mapping and navigating information space." Using an effective search strategy, the investigator locates suitable resources, evaluates them for appropriateness by considering copyright dates and viewpoints, then accesses the information through indexes, cross-references, electronic search strategies, etc.

With Dan's Generic Model, students "seek and access" information from various sources. Students access not only traditional reference materials but also primary documents, experts, and multimedia resources. They may even use personal observations. An emphasis on primary sources, including personal observations and interviews with experts, elevates the process from re-searching to original searching. Teachers and library media specialists work with students before allowing them to approach and interview professionals, however. Students are taught to show respect for these experts' knowledge and time and to show consideration for both by being prepared for the interview. Students are encouraged to gather enough foundation knowledge from general sources beforehand so that they can intelligently discuss the topic and ask appropriate questions.

One of the best methods of teaching this phase of the research process is modeling effective information-seeking strategies. Teachers and library media specialists foster information literacy skills and abilities in their students when they "think aloud" as they demonstrate locating and accessing information.

> *The class of first-graders completed their presearch, formulated five questions they wanted answered, went to the museum, and interviewed the curator. They are now ready to go to the library media center and look up more information on dinosaurs. In the library media center, the library media specialist and the teacher talk about what information the students are looking for. The library media specialist talks about encyclopedias and what kind of information is found there. The library media center is fortunate to have several sets of animal encyclopedias and the students start their research by looking in these. They also look up information on the CD-ROM encyclopedias, and print out pictures of their favorite dinosaurs. Instead of preparing individual reports, the students are writing one report that answers their five questions.*

Understanding and Appraising Information

Choosing, selecting, and evaluating information are some of the activities students will be involved in during this stage of the research process. InfoZone advises students to concentrate on the chosen topic and to notice whether sources agree or disagree when they are "choosing" resources and information. Organized Investigators "consume and gulp" information during this phase by "reading, viewing, listening, observing, collecting, and computing." They skim their material for keywords, then evaluate it for accuracy, relevance, and reliability. Keeping only pertinent information, they check for viewpoint, bias, fact or opinion, or errors in logic. Finally, they "do mental battle with the ideas encountered, rejecting some, none, or all ideas." Similarly, in the Pathways to Knowledge "interpretation" stage, students assess what they have found, and then interpret useful information by inferring, analyzing, and paraphrasing.

Students engage in "sorting and sifting" information in The Research Cycle. They take advantage of the benefits of technology by keeping found information in databases or word processing files. After analyzing the information, students discard the "info-garbage" and, using computer capabilities, rearrange the "meaningful and reliable data" so that they make sense and throw light on the essential question.

The skill of appraising information has never been as important as it is now with the abundance of information available on the Internet and in the media. Neither are controlled environments and both offer accurate and inaccurate, biased and unbiased, easily accessible information. As Dan's Generic Model states, students must "select" information and then "evaluate" it according to accuracy and relevance. The ability to recognize the good and the bad and then discriminate between them is necessary in today's information age. Teachers and library media specialists foster this aspect of information literacy by discussing and demonstrating its importance, by providing evaluation guidelines, and by leading students through the appraisal process.

> *The students looked in nonfiction books, encyclopedias, and CD-ROM encyclopedias and talked with a museum curator. Now they take all the information and discuss it with the teacher and library media specialist. They consider the questions one by one, and decide which information, from which source, best answers that question. During this process, the teacher and library media specialist ask the questions and then question the students' responses. This give-and-take process refines the information and breaks it down into facts the students can understand. This is the basis of their report. (This is an example of the use of information in the Big6™ model.)*

Organizing and Using Information

The Big6 Skills™ Approach refers to this stage as "synthesis." The model's definition of synthesis includes the "restructuring or repackaging of information into new or different formats to meet the requirements of the task." Using databases, note cards, or graphic organizers, students organize information from several sources so that it makes sense.

In The Research Cycle, students "synthesize" information to help them in making decisions or solving problems. This model suggests students use the SCAMPER process to aid in this endeavor. SCAMPER refers to Substitute, Combine, Adapt, Modify, Magnify, Minify, Put to other uses, Eliminate, and Reverse. Employing these strategies helps students "envision" possibilities and "invent" answers to their essential questions.

Dan's Generic Model suggests that students "synthesize" information by "bringing all of the threads related to the concept or question together to form a pattern of understanding and a direction for continued growth." This idea is emphasized in the InfoZone model as well. InfoZone's "connecting" likens integrating information to weaving fabric, and promotes the use of graphic organizers such as webs, charts, timelines, or tables. These tools help students identify and discard duplicate, unwanted, or irrelevant material.

Pathways to Knowledge includes the organizing step in their communications strand. Students organize and format information in a variety of ways. In doing so, they are "constructing new knowledge" or adding to what they already know. The Organized Investigator elaborates on this concept by stating that students in this stage draw conclusions or solve problems based on their new knowledge.

Organizing information and connecting newfound information in ways that make sense are difficult tasks for students to tackle on their own. Teachers and library media specialists facilitate the process by introducing and demonstrating the use of databases and other graphic organizers and modeling the thought processes that go into deciding which graphic organizer will be most effective. For example, databases are very helpful when the information is to be compared, analyzed, sorted, or re-sorted to show different connections. In addition, although timelines are great for organizing information in chronological order, and webs are good for identifying major topics and discovering related ideas, an outline may be best for organizing information for a written report. More important, though, teachers and library media specialists need to remember that even the brightest student is not born knowing how to organize information—how to develop a web, create a database, or draw a timeline. These are information literacy skills that must be taught by demonstrating, modeling, and giving students plenty of practice and experience working with them.

> *Now that the students have asked and answered their questions, they draw a web, with the word* dinosaur *in the middle. They then draw lines to five boxes, each of which contains one of the questions they want answered. As they perform this task, they discuss all the information they have gathered and learned about dinosaurs. From each question box, they draw more lines and box in answers to the specific questions.*

Communicating Information

InfoZone describes this stage as "producing," because students are producing a variety of information products to communicate what they have learned. When deciding which product will be most effective, students should consider the audience, the message, and what format will best show what they have learned. The Organized Investigator also "communicates" by selecting a presentation format appropriate for the audience and the purpose of the research. Emphasis is placed on documenting sources in this phase.

"Communication" is the term used by Pathways to Knowledge for the phase in which students share their new knowledge by "speaking, writing, creating, designing, and demonstrating." The Big6 Skills™ Approach asks the question, "What can I make to show what I learned?" and suggests using a variety of media. Called "reporting" by The Research Cycle, this is the step in which the "researcher translates findings into a persuasive, instructive or effective product."

Students "communicate, repackage, and apply" information in this phase of Dan's Generic Model. The process consists of repackaging information so that it can be used to solve problems or to make decisions, and includes selecting the best method of communicating the results of the search.

> *The library media specialist has two books of dinosaur masks. The children are delighted! They pick out one to wear—but first they must tell the library media specialist what kind of dinosaur it is and one fact about that dinosaur. This becomes their report. Each child wears a mask and reports the facts he or she has learned about that particular dinosaur. The narrator gives an overall introduction and supplies facts about the earth during the time of the dinosaurs. At the end of the class report, students take turns to talk about why dinosaurs no longer exist on earth.*

Evaluating the Process and the Product

All the research models stress evaluating the process as well as the product. The Organized Investigator "reflects" on the process and product and asks, "How well did I do and how could I do better right now?" More specifically, evaluation of the process is an ongoing activity with students revising strategies or changing goals as needed. Process evaluation includes determining how well the search met the information need or solved the problem. The students reflect on the new knowledge and skills they have acquired. The Pathways to Knowledge "Evaluation" strand goes one step further and instructs students to think about how they would change their strategies for subsequent searches. Students who are working through The Research Cycle keep journals that explain the reasoning behind their strategies. These journals are reviewed at the end of the year by the teacher and library media specialist in an effort to evaluate the students' levels of information literacy skills and the effectiveness of the information literacy instruction.

InfoZone's "Judging" process urges students to look for the strengths and weaknesses in their project, think about what worked and what didn't, and consider what advice they would give someone else tackling the same project. The Big6™ approach was the first to focus on evaluating both the process and the product. In its evaluation step, The Big6 Skills™ Approach directs students to answer the question, "How will I know I did my job well?" by judging the product for effectiveness and judging the information problem-solving process for efficiency. In addition to deciding if the need was met and the problem solved, students are urged to consider how long the process took to complete. How much actual time was spent on successful activities? Did it take longer than they thought? Through this self-examination, students will improve their information literacy skills.

"Reflection" is also a part of Dan's Generic Model. Students reflect on their entire research experiences beginning with what they knew (prior knowledge) and what they wanted to learn. They also reflect on their research strategies and whether or not they were successful. Thoughtful reflection can turn even unsuccessful searches into valuable lessons by allowing students to discover the limitations of some searching strategies and also to learn from their mistakes.

Evaluation of a research project is often done solely by the teacher. Occasionally the library media specialist assists in evaluating the unit as a whole and recommending improvements. As these models suggest, however, it is important that students be involved in the evaluation procedure as well. When students are taught to critique their own finished products for accuracy of information, relevancy to the topic, completeness of coverage, appropriateness of the presentation format, and appearance of the overall project, they learn how to work independently and how to judge their own work without depending on grades or the opinions of others. When students are taught to reflect on their own information-seeking methods and to devise strategies to improve them, they refine their skills and begin to take responsibility for their own learning. They become information literate!

> *The teacher and the media specialist are very proud of the children! This process was driven solely by the students' interest in dinosaurs. When asked what they thought about the process, the children wished they could have talked to more experts about dinosaurs.*

Formulating New Questions

This last stage gets its name from Information Literacy: Dan's Generic Model. Barron refers to it as the "never-ending story" of questioning, discovery, and questioning again, even after the research project is complete. It also is implied by the Organized Investigator's circular model, where the last step, "reflects," points once again toward the first step, "questions and wonders." The title of The Research Cycle illustrates the importance of the cyclical approach to questioning, evaluating, and requestioning throughout the process. As with "appreciating and enjoying information" at the beginning, this final stage is often overlooked and undervalued. Intriguing research projects cause students to ask even more questions. Teachers and library media specialists need to encourage this curiosity by allowing students time to follow their interests. It is through this course that independent learners—and experts—are born.

Evaluating the Researcher

Several of the research models include rubrics to evaluate students' information literacy skills. Jamieson McKenzie and the Oak Harbor Schools created the Information Skills Rating Scale[7] to assess how well students completed the steps in The Research Cycle. The rating scale lists three levels of information literacy for each stage of The Research Cycle. The level of least ability is numbered 1, the middle level is numbered 3, and the highest skill level is given a 5. For example, the skill associated with "Sorting" is "reorganizes information so that the most valuable becomes readily available to support understanding." A level-1 researcher "leaves information as gathered." A level-3 researcher "creates partial organization of information." A fully developed level-5 researcher "creates structure which provides a coherent and clear focus."

The Big6 Skills™ Approach to Library and Information Instruction stresses the importance of a project-specific assessment guide that considers each step in the research process. The "Big6™ Scoring Guide"[8] offers teachers an "effective, easy-to-use tool to help with assessment." The teacher uses this guide with students to communicate what is expected and to evaluate students' progress during each stage of the research process. The "Scoring Guide" lists the stages of the research process and specifies what outcome is required for the rating of highly competent, competent, adequate, or not yet acceptable. The particular product or activity that will be used as evidence of the students' information-seeking skills is also specified. Because every project does not necessarily stress or include every stage of the information-seeking process, the teacher decides which skills to focus on and assigns appropriate percentage points to each. The developers of the scoring guide emphasize evaluating the research process through qualitative criteria rather than through quantitative measures. They also state that the guides are "useful both during and after working on assignments—for both formative and summative assessment." Students are not necessarily at the same stage of development for each skill; they may be fairly competent at locating, accessing, and using information, but unskilled at synthesizing and presenting it. For this reason, teachers and library media specialists need to monitor all students during each phase of the research process.

Another evaluation rubric, designed by the California Technology Assistance Program, Region VII, offers developmental benchmarks for information literacy development.[9] This rubric lists seven characteristics of beginner, intermediate, and advanced information-literate students. The beginner level lists characteristics such as "has little or no experience using a wide variety of information sources" and "requires a great deal of teacher direction and support." An intermediate-level student "has experience using a few information sources well," but "is easily frustrated as the project develops." An advanced information-literate student is "a critical thinker," an "interested learner," and an "organized investigator." In addition to the student characteristics listed, the benchmarks include the types of information sources to be used with each level and the help and guidance that should be offered at each stage. Beginner researchers should be "guided to a limited number of preselected sources" (Types of Information Sources) and should be "closely monitor[ed] . . . as they encounter information" (Help and Guidance). Information sources for intermediate researchers should be "complex enough that persistence and skill are required to yield results (may require two-step lookup)." Teachers and library media specialists should "assist students in recognizing and filtering for relevant information." Advanced students are able to handle sources that "contain a variety of viewpoints and perspectives." For these students, teachers and library media specialists should "encourage use of the full range of information sources and technologies" and "provide more sophisticated searching strategies." Because most elementary students are at the beginner or intermediate levels of information literacy development, teachers and library media specialists need to monitor closely the information sources being used and the instruction and guidance being offered.

THE OTHER ESSENTIALS

Instruction and practice in using the research process are necessary requirements for an information literacy program. Other essential components include the philosophies and teaching strategies that support and foster information literacy instruction. All the subject-area standards, as well as the information literacy standards, focus on the student as an active learner, not a passive receptacle of facts. Active learning translates into hands-on experiences with an abundant variety of information sources. This requires that instruction be resource-based and not limited to textbooks. Textbooks may be used as a resource, but should not be the only source of information. Diaries, original documents, newspaper and magazine articles, reference books, nonfiction books, experts, videos, museums, maps, charts, the Internet, works of art, plays, CD-ROMs, musical compositions, poems, and even games should be among the many resources available to students as they seek to gather information, to create knowledge, and to increase their skills.

Information literacy also demands the ability to think critically and to solve problems. Students' future successes, both in school and in life, depend on the development of these skills. A problem-solving curriculum based on real, authentic concerns, or interests, provides instruction and practice in these skills. This type of curriculum has the added benefit of being a great motivator for reluctant learners. The art of teaching problem-solving skills is discussed further in chapter 6. Critical-thinking skills are considered in depth in chapter 7.

Authentic, problem-solving research activities do not fit nicely and easily into one discipline. They branch out to include information from all subject areas. They resemble life, where social studies teachings combine with math and science skills, language arts abilities, and fine arts creativity to provide awareness and solutions for problems such as the overpopulation of the world, or the overflowing of a county-owned drainage ditch. If students are to become information literate—if they are to understand the words, signs, and symbols of the world they live in, and are to use and communicate this knowledge—then teachers and library media specialists need to show them how all the parts are connected. For this reason, teachers and library media specialists are urged to cooperate and collaborate on integrated, interdisciplinary curriculum units.

SUMMARY

The essential components of an effective information literacy program include instruction and practice in the research process, a resource-based curriculum, and opportunities to engage in critical thinking and problem solving. All these components are connected through an interdisciplinary unit approach to teaching and learning.

The research process is comprised of the following steps: Appreciating/ Enjoying Information, Wondering, Background Building, Seeking Information, Understanding and Appraising Information, Organizing and Using Information, Communicating Information, Evaluating the Process and the Product, and Formulating New Questions. Although the steps are listed in linear form, actual research rarely follows a straight path but is full of twists and turns and circle-backs.

Teachers and library media specialists should use evaluation rubrics to assess students' levels of information literacy and the effectiveness of information literacy instruction. It also is essential that students be a part of the evaluation process and use rubrics to critique their own research techniques as well as the products they have created. This activity helps students form accurate judgments of their own work and become responsible for their own learning.

NOTES

1. Michael Eisenberg and Robert Berkowitz, *Information Problem-Solving: The Big6 Skills™ Approach to Library and Information Skills Instruction* (Norwood, NJ: Ablex, 1990); Michael Eisenberg and Robert Berkowitz, 1998, *The Big6.com Teaching Technology & Information Skills*. URL: http://big6.com. (Accessed November 9, 1999). The six steps in the Information Problem Solving process are listed as 1) Task Definition, 2) Information-Seeking Strategies, 3) Location and Access, 4) Use of Information, 5) Synthesis, and 6) Evaluation. Each big step is defined by two activities. These are sometimes called "the little twelve." For younger students, the Big6™ steps are listed as questions to facilitate understanding. They are 1) What is my question? Is it a good question? 2) How can I get my information? 3) Where can I find this information? 4) How can I use this information? 5) What can I make to show what I learned? and 6) How will I know I did my job well? The Big6 Skills™ program is a problem-solving approach to library and information skills instruction. In addition to listing the skills and the evaluation rubric, the Web site offers an online newsletter, a listserv, examples of the skills approach in action, and links to related sites.

2.   Marg Stimson, 1998, *InfoZone*. URL: http://www.assd.winnipeg.mb.ca/infozone/ index.htm. (Accessed November 9, 1999). Reprinted by permission. This site is designed for students and other people interested in learning how to go about research. The steps included in this model are "Wondering: Defining the Need for Information," "Seeking: Locating and Accessing Resources," "Choosing: Understanding and Appraising Information," "Connecting: Organizing Information," "Producing: Communicating the Information," and "Judging: Evaluating the Process and Product." Beneath each step are links to sites that will aid students (and others) in completing that step. For instance, the links under "Wondering" contain sources of interest-grabbing research topics. Each step also details "Things to Think About" when working on that phase. The "Judging" section includes a valuable and easily understood checklist for students to use in evaluating each phase of their research project and suggests people who might give additional feedback on the finished product.

3.   Follett Software Company, 1998, *Pathways to Knowledge*. URL: http://www. pathwaysmodel.com/. (Accessed November 9, 1999). Reprinted by permission. Pathways to Knowledge: Follett's Information Skills Model is deliberately nonlinear to show that searchers can begin the process at any stage and follow a variety of paths. The graphic version of the model depicts strands (steps) or expanding ripples that contain examples of resources, activities, or thinking processes associated with that strand. The wide variety of samples takes into account individual learning styles and differing search strategies. The broad strands are Appreciation/Enjoyment, Presearch, Search, Interpretation, Communication, and Evaluation.

4.   David V. Loertscher, n.d., *Organized Investigator*. URL: http://ctap.fcoe.k12.ca.us/ ctap/Info.Lit/Organized.html. (Accessed November 9, 1999). This circular model, contributed by Dr. David V. Loertscher, is included in the California Technology Assistance Program's Information Literacy Web pages. It features a circle with the student in the center and the research process outlined on the circumference. Arrows radiate back and forth between the student and each stage of the process and between adjoining stages. Designed to illustrate paths researchers follow, the circular model highlights the idea that not all paths are similar, nor linear, nor the same every time, nor for every person, but all include certain stages or steps that must be accomplished if the researcher is successful. Beginning at the top of the circle, the steps shown are Questions and Wonders, Finds and Sorts, Consumes and Gulps, Thinks and Creates, Summarizes and Concludes, Communicates, and Reflects on Process and Product.

5.   Jamieson McKenzie, 1997, *The Research Cycle Revisited*. URL: http://www.fno.org/ oct97/research.html. (Accessed November 9, 1999). Reprinted by permission. Developed by Jamieson McKenzie, The Research Cycle offers teachers and library media specialists an outline for guiding students through the research process. The term *cycle* implies that the process does not end but repeats itself continuously. The steps include Questioning, Planning, Gathering, Sorting and Sifting, Synthesizing, Evaluating, and Reporting. This site provides a short version and a more in-depth explanation of The Research Cycle.

6.   Daniel D. Barron, personal e-mail, November 20, 1998. Dr. Barron is a professor and coordinator of the School Library Media Program at the College of Library and Information Science at the University of South Carolina. Dr. Barron's generic model follows the basic steps outlined in the other models. However, it does not end with the

evaluation procedure, but specifically states that students should be encouraged to ask even more questions. Known as Information Literacy: Dan's Generic Model, the process contains the following steps: 1) Formulate a Question; 2) Access/Seek Information; 3) Select Information; 4) Evaluate Information; 5) Synthesize Information; 6) Communicate/ Repackage/Apply Information; and 7) Reflect/Evaluate/Formulate Other Questions.

7.   Jamieson McKenzie, 1997, *The Oak Harbor, Washington Information Skills Rating Scale*. URL: http://www.fno.org/libskill.html. (Accessed November 8, 1999). The Oak Harbor, Washington, Information Skills Rating Scale was created to help teachers and library media specialists assess the level of students' abilities in The Research Cycle. The scale lists and defines the components of the cycle, then gives indicators of high-, medium-, and low-level skills for each one. High-level abilities are given a rating of 5 on the scale. Medium levels are 3 and low levels are rated 1. Students' total scores can be interpreted as indicators of their overall strength in information seeking.

8.   Michael Eisenberg and Robert Berkowitz, "Assessment: Big6™ Scoring Guides for Diagnosis and Prescription," *Information and Technology Skills for Students' Success: The Big6 Skills™ Approach* (1997): 85–87. This assessment guide was developed as a tool for teachers, students, and library media specialists to use in evaluating the research process. It is intended to be used for both formative and summative assessment. Formative assessments, performed during the learning experience, reveal gaps in students' abilities in time for teachers and library media specialists to make adjustments in teaching techniques or emphases. The "Big6™ Scoring Guide" article was published in the *Big6™* newsletter.

9.   From California Technology Assistance Program, n.d., *Information Literacy Developmental Benchmarks*. URL: http://ctap.fcoe.k12.ca.us/ctap/Info.Lit/Benchmarks.html. (Accessed November 8, 1999). Reprinted by permission. This useful document provides teachers and library media specialists with benchmarks for evaluating students' information literacy development, and also describes the kind of resources and amount of guidance appropriate for each level. The chart lists seven Student Characteristics for Beginner, Intermediate, and Advanced levels, and states the Types of Information Sources and the Help and Guidance needed for each.

ADDITIONAL READINGS

Eisenberg, Michael B., and Robert E. Berkowitz. "The Six Habits of Highly Effective Students: Using the Big6™ to Link Parents, Students, and Homework." *School Library Journal* (August 1995): 22–25. Written by the developers of the Big6™ Skills Approach to Information Problem Solving, this article translates the six questions or skills into steps parents can follow to help their children with homework assignments.

Freeman, Greg. N.d. *The Graphic Organizer*. URL: http://www.graphic.org/. Accessed November 8, 1999. This interesting site has many links to information about graphic organizers, examples of how to use graphic organizers, and guidelines for designing them.

Kuhlthau, Carol C. 1996. *The Concept of a Zone of Intervention for Identifying the Role of Intermediaries in the Information Search Process*. URL: http://www.asis.org/ annual-96/ElectronicProceedings/kuhlthau.html. Accessed November 8, 1999. Click on link to Electronic Proceedings. Then click on Information Search Process. Presented at the ASIS 1996 Annual Conference, this paper discusses the zone of intervention in relation to a researcher and the research process. The zone of intervention is described as that time in which the researcher can go forward with help, but is frustrated or confused on his or her own. The article notes that if offered too early, help is unwanted. If offered too late, help is overwhelming.

Parks, Sandra, and Howard Black. *Organizing Thinking, Book I*. Pacific Grove, CA: Critical Thinking Press & Software, 1992. This book on graphic organizers contains black-line masters of specific graphic organizers and examples of how they can be used in all subject-area lessons.

Chapter **5**

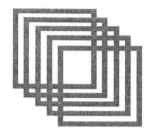

The Necessary Reforms and Changing Responsibilities

New opinions are always suspected, and usually opposed, without any other reason but because they are not already common.

—John Locke

The previous chapters have alluded to educational philosophies and practices that foster the teaching and learning of information literacy. What has not been mentioned is that information literacy instruction depends upon the acceptance of changing views of education and changing methods of teaching. Because change, like new opinions, is always "suspected," teachers and library media specialists who wish to implement new information literacy strategies may encounter resistance from board members, administrators, colleagues, parents, and some students. Although not entirely new—wise teachers have recognized them for centuries[1]—these ideas are not yet common. The rest of this chapter provides some background on the changing views of education and explains the resulting changes in teaching practices that are required for information literacy instruction.

CHANGING VIEWS OF EDUCATION

That education has changed from the one-room classroom where students recited their lessons out loud comes as no surprise to anyone. How students actually learn and what they should be learning may surprise many. Research in brain development, multiple intelligences, and learning styles has caused educators to rethink how students should be taught. The increasing and ever-changing amount of information being discovered has caused societies to rethink what they want students to learn. The combination of the two points to fundamental changes in the daily life of the school. The following viewpoints are adapted from *The Information Literacy Blueprint,* developed by Griffin University,[2] "Changing Emphases" from the National Science Education Standards,[3] and "Next Steps" from the National Council of Teachers of Mathematics Standards.[4]

Changing Views of Learning

At one time, students learned a body of constant facts that could be memorized and retained for all time. Learning was a stable product to own or a destination to achieve. For the most part, learning stopped when schooling stopped. Today, the emphasis is on students learning how to learn—becoming information literate—so they can keep abreast of the changes in information and technology and be able to adapt to new situations. Learning is now perceived as a process, not a product; people do not quit learning when they leave school, but remain lifelong learners.

Changing Views of Curriculum

Once, curriculum objectives deemed appropriate for certain age groups or grade levels were specified and inflexible. Year after year, all students in a particular grade studied a set outline of subject matter. Now objectives are flexible, taking individual and cultural differences into account. Students are sometimes grouped by abilities, not always age, and subject matter is matched accordingly.[5] Current events, local resources, and students' interests are also taken into account as curriculum objectives are adjusted to make learning more relevant.

Changing Views of Classrooms

Classrooms were originally designed for the convenience of the teacher and the lecture method of teaching. A teacher's desk, a chalkboard, students' desks arranged in straight rows and facing forward, a bulletin board, and possibly a map or globe were the only essential items in a classroom. Today, the classroom is viewed as an environment where active learning takes place. Overhead projectors, television monitors, VCRs, and computers are standard equipment in most classrooms. Desks, or tables, are arranged or grouped according to the activity involved.

Manipulatives and other learning objects are abundant. The classroom environment is conducive to learning and encourages students to become self-disciplined, self-reliant, and responsible for their own learning.

Changing Views of Information

Information used to be seen as a static and constant object, with identical meaning for everyone. It was passed from teachers to students with little regard for understanding or usefulness. Educators today realize that information means different things to different people. They realize that students need to be actively involved in seeking information and using it in some way as they create their own unique concepts of knowledge based on previous understandings and experiences. This new view helps students realize that information creates meaning and understanding and that gathering information can help them make sense of their surroundings.

Changing Views of Students

Students were long viewed as passive receptacles of information whose main responsibility was to listen, remember, and later repeat the information they heard. Students had no control over what they "learned" or how they were tested. All students were expected to conform to the standard idea of a good learner. Those who did were rewarded with good treatment and the teacher's recognition. Differences were discouraged; those who were different were often punished. Students today are viewed as information seekers, information users, decision makers, and problem solvers. What they learn depends on what they need to know to make a decision or to solve a problem. Differences are adjusted to and often taken advantage of, and all students are treated with respect.

Changing Views of Teachers

Teachers were once merely givers of information. They taught by talking. Students learned by listening. Isolated from colleagues and other professionals by classroom walls, grade-level separations, and curriculum restrictions, teachers worked alone when planning and teaching. Now teachers are facilitators of the learning process and are constantly learning, too. Learning becomes an experience that teachers and students share with each other. Teachers are no longer isolated, but work collaboratively with other teachers, library media specialists, community members, and even (via the Internet) other educators throughout the world.

Changing Views of Assessments

Traditionally, students' learning was assessed by written tests—usually multiple choice, matching, or short answer. Sometimes a discussion question or two was included to engage higher-order thinking skills and check for understanding. Students also were graded on homework, class work (mostly worksheets), and occasionally a written report. These grades were shown as letters or numbers on a report card and then were dismissed. They were merely representations of how well students could repeat what they had been told. Science projects that showed information being used were the exception. Now projects of all sorts are the rule. Authentic assessments are intended to gauge what students learn by measuring how well they use the information. Portfolios of multimedia projects, presentations of solutions to problems, and written reports that include why and how the information was found, as well as what was found, are all examples of authentic assessments.[6] The changing views of assessment include not only the way students are assessed but also how this information is used. When teachers assess how students learn as well as what they learn, they can adjust teaching methods to "improve instruction, learning, and programs" (NCTM Standards, "Next Steps," "Concluding Comments").

Changing Views of
Libraries and Librarians

School libraries were designed long ago as storehouses of books and were arranged for convenient, efficient storage. Librarians were seen as the "keepers of the books" and guardians of the libraries. It was often assumed that school librarians cared more about the books than they did about the students who read them. Librarians had minimal contact with students, usually through a fixed schedule of thirty- or forty-minute increments once every week or two weeks. During this time, librarians read stories or taught library skills in isolation and students checked out books. School library media centers now are places where information can be found not just in books but also in videos, audio recordings, pictures, and photographs, CD-ROMs, the Internet, models, maps, etc. Library media centers are designed to provide not only efficient storage but also equal access to information and the convenient retrieval of it. Library media specialists keep the books and other information resources, and also instruct students in accessing, evaluating, organizing, and using information and creating information products. Library media specialists now work cooperatively with teachers to plan units that integrate information literacy skills into subject-area curricula. In most instances, they see classes through a flexible schedule that adapts to the information needs of the students and teachers. An inviting library media center and a vibrant library media program today are viewed as integral components of an effective school.

CHANGING METHODS OF TEACHING

The changing views of education that correspond with the need for information literacy instruction require a transformation in the way we teach. As our understandings adjust to include new knowledge of how students learn and what they need to learn, our methods of teaching must adapt as well. Our old methods are not necessarily wrong—they worked well with a majority of students for several generations—but they are obsolete.[7] The world is different now. People are different, families are different, society is different, and students are different. What once worked well will no longer do the job. That is evident from low standardized test scores, high dropout rates, an underskilled workforce, and a growing number of unemployable citizens. Educational reform is necessary. But what and how?

The reforms needed are design changes—fundamental alterations in the way we do things to solve persistent problems (NCTM Standards, "Next Steps," "The Nature of Change"). Research on multiple intelligences and learning styles points to changes in the way information is delivered and received. Cooperative and interpersonal skills required in the workplace direct a change in the way students work. An emphasis on systems and understanding the integrated whole as well as the individual parts leads to a change in the way subject matter is presented. The identification of information literacy skills needed for lifelong learning and thinking promotes a change in what is taught. Brain-based research that shows how students learn dictates a change in how teachers teach. The abundance of information in all formats necessitates a change in the information resources teachers and students use and the strategies needed to access and evaluate them.

The following chart (table 5.1) from an AASL teleconference on information literacy, depicts the old methods of teaching and the new methods that have taken their place.[8]

Table 5.1
Old Teaching Methods (Left) Compared to New Methods

CHANGING PARADIGMS

Lecture/Listen	Actively Engaged
Individual Effort	Group Effort
Subjects	Integration
Facts	Problem Centered
Sage on the Stage	Guide on the Side
Spoken/Written	All Resources
RRR (42 hours)	Authentic/Portfolio
Insular Programs	Community Collaboration

The changes mentioned above must be implemented if information literacy instruction is to become a part of the daily life of the school.

WHO DOES WHAT?

Reform carries responsibility. For information literacy instruction to be effective, everyone in the school community needs to become involved. Administrators, teachers, parents, families, students, and library media specialists contribute to information literacy goals by actively participating in school-wide reforms and implementation processes.

Administrators

Administrators foster information literacy by providing support—support in funding, planning, and scheduling. Administrators establish the priorities that are the basis for decisions concerning how money is spent, when planning is accomplished, and how the school day is scheduled. To foster information literacy, these priorities need to ensure adequate information resources and personnel for the library media center, adequate planning time for teachers and the library media specialist, and flexible scheduling for the library media center.

Funding

Information literacy instruction is dependent upon an abundant supply of various information resources: books, videos, CD-ROMs, Internet sites, photographs, maps, periodicals, databases, artifacts, etc. Students cannot learn how to find and evaluate information from a variety of sources if they do not have access to these sources. Administrators must be willing to allocate funds to provide an information-rich environment for students to explore and learn to manage.

Administrators also must be willing to hire professional library media specialists (to supervise the library media program) and assistants (to help run the library media center). Library media specialists are experts in selecting information resources, in working with students, and in collaborating with teachers. This expertise is wasted and entire information literacy programs are compromised if library media specialists spend the majority of their time checking out books, checking in books, and shelving them again. Paraprofessionals who assist with these and other tasks are crucial to the success of an information literacy program.

Planning

Another essential component of an information literacy program is cooperative planning and discussion—both among teachers and between library media specialists and teachers. Teachers and library media specialists need time to plan thematic units, evaluate teaching strategies, assess student progress in information literacy development, and share new information and ideas. Administrators facilitate this process by providing time during the daily schedule for joint planning and sharing.

Scheduling

A third necessary component of information literacy instruction is scheduling for the flexible use of the library media center. This is, perhaps, the most difficult task elementary school administrators face when implementing a school-wide information literacy program. It is, however, essential. Flexible scheduling allows students and teachers access to the library media center's resources when the resources are most essential—when an information need arises.[9] Although most elementary school principals agree to the principle of flexible scheduling, many do not know how to accomplish it. Traditionally, library time for students provided planning time for teachers. It is possible, however, to schedule for both, as many administrators and faculties have discovered. Some schools have an exploratory computer class or science lab that takes the place of library time. Others schedule two or more art, music, or physical education classes per week. Flexible scheduling is practiced in many elementary school library media centers. It can be done and should be adopted in all library media centers to help foster information literacy.

Teachers

Information literacy skills cannot be taught solely in the library media center; they must be introduced and practiced daily in the classroom as well. Teachers foster information literacy by engaging students in thoughtful, authentic learning experiences using a wide variety of information sources, by providing guidance in the research process, and by modeling information literacy skills and thinking processes.

Thoughtful Learning Experiences

Incorporating information literacy objectives into lesson plans is not a difficult task. As illustrated in chapter 3, information literacy skills are included in all the national curriculum standards—math, science, English language arts, social studies, and fine arts. Teachers easily can include information literacy objectives in subject-area lessons by planning hands-on, resource-based, problem-solving activities for students. Hands-on activities increase students' involvement in the learning process. Learning that is resource-based provides information-seeking, evaluating, and organizing opportunities. Authentic problem-solving activities add meaning to students' learning experiences, illustrate the real-life need for information literacy skills, and give practice in critical and creative thinking.[10] Chapter 8 includes a checklist of information literacy skills along with the specific activities that foster them.

Homework plays a big part in the daily life of both the school and the students. Teachers foster information literacy by creating homework assignments that combine real-life activities with skills learned in school. For instance, instead of assigning a page of fraction problems, ask students to convert a recipe for six servings to one that serves eighteen. Some students could even bake enough cookies for the whole class.[11] Homework activities like these emphasize an authentic need for skills while providing practice in using the skills. Other homework assignments may require interaction between students and parents. For example, have students ask their parents how they decided what type of car to buy, or where to go on vacation, or which brand of detergent to use. Find out what information they needed to make a decision, how and where they found this information, and how they evaluated it. Homework assignments can foster information literacy by reinforcing the idea that information literacy skills are needed in everyday life.

Research Guidance

As mentioned in chapter 4, students need guidance in the research process. Teachers make this easier by collaborating with the library media specialist to introduce the steps of the research process and to help instruct students in the skills needed. Many of the steps in the information-seeking process will be performed in the library media center. Others, such as organizing or synthesizing information, can be accomplished in the classroom. Teachers need to discuss with students the different processes involved in these activities as well as the information found.

Modeling

Students learn from observing how teachers think and function. Consequently, the behavior of teachers is reflected in the behavior of students.[12] Teachers who model information literacy skills will have students who imitate them. Modeling can be used as a deliberate teaching strategy during an introductory activity, as a quick reminder of previous skills learned, or in a one-on-one musing of actual problem-solving thought processes. Deliberate modeling shows students how a resource is used (such as an index or catalog) or how a strategy is carried out (such as narrowing a topic or webbing). Teachers go through the processes exactly as the students should, step by step. When modeling is used as a reminder or reinforcement of previously learned skills, teachers may ask such questions as, "I need to find some information on whales. Where should I look first?" or "I found a book on birds. How can I find out if it has information on owls?" The third type of modeling is used in response to an actual information question. Teachers think aloud as they ponder the question and come up with suggestions or solutions to the problem. Modeling in these situations demonstrates information literacy skills in action—as they are needed and used in real life. Teachers foster information literacy by modeling the thinking and the skills involved.

Parents and Families

Parents are not only their children's first teachers, they are their constant teachers. As such, they are the most influential and have the greatest, lasting impact on student learning. Families have many opportunities to foster information literacy skills.[13] One of the best ways to encourage information literacy is to encourage reading. This can be done by providing abundant appropriate reading materials, spending time reading with children, and reading for personal information and pleasure. Giving children their own subscriptions to magazines is a wonderful way to encourage reading. *Highlights*,[14] *Cricket*,[15] *Cobblestone*,[16] and *Crinkles*[17] are some of the many high-quality magazines developed specifically for children. *Crinkles* ("Because learning makes crinkles in your brain!") is a library media magazine for kids. It fosters information literacy development by encouraging children to read further and research topics discussed in the magazine. Many activities in the magazine rely on children to read and to gather information from outside sources. Because most information resources require the ability to read, learning to read well is necessary for information literacy. Parents and families who encourage reading are helping their children become information-literate lifelong learners.

Modeling and discussing information-seeking skills are other methods of fostering information literacy. When faced with the decision of which television to purchase or the problem of fixing a leaky toilet, think out loud and discuss the information choices and solutions available. Demonstrating the full spectrum of information literacy skills, as they are used in real life, is an excellent way to nurture their development.

Families can further the development of information literacy by playing games or sharing other thinking activities with their children. A "think and win" strategy shows information being used in critical thinking and problem solving. Families also can encourage children to pursue their hobbies or interests and to use the research process to gather information on these topics. Showing information literacy "in action" is one of the most valuable ways families can contribute to an information literacy program.

Students

Students are partners in the learning process. As partners in their own learning, students have a responsibility to come to school prepared to learn, to be willing to learn, to cooperate with their teachers and peers, to complete assignments, and to participate in learning activities. Students who realize early that they are responsible for their own learning will acquire the information literacy skills and abilities to become lifelong learners.

Library Media Specialists

Library media specialists are leaders in the information literacy movement and as such will be leaders in school-wide information literacy implementation programs. Although other educators acknowledge the importance of information literacy instruction, librarians are the first to develop standards and indicators for information literacy goals and objectives. Therefore, library media specialists must take the initiative to introduce the standards to the school community and to coordinate the adoption of a school-wide program. This book was developed to ease the process by providing library media specialists the information and tools needed to introduce, justify, and coordinate a school-wide information literacy instruction program.

Introducing

Library media specialists can introduce the concept of information literacy to the faculty through in-services, formal and informal planning sessions, and casual conversations. The concept can be reinforced through ongoing conversations, planning sessions, and dissemination of articles concerning information literacy.

Parents also need to be informed about the school's information literacy emphasis. This can be done through PTSA (Parent Teacher Student Association) meetings, parenting sessions, and newsletters. Again, the library media specialist probably will be the spokesperson for these activities as well.

Transparency masters and a handout for an information literacy in-service for teachers are provided in appendixes F and G. These in-service tools include a definition of information literacy, some justifications for teaching it, and a few implementation suggestions. The in-service is designed to be a starting point for further discussions and eventual joint planning sessions.

Justifying

It is important to demonstrate to teachers the significance of information literacy instruction. The background information and the supporting documents mentioned in chapter 2 will help library media specialists with this task. Along with justifying information literacy, library media specialists also may need to justify the instructional changes needed to implement a school-wide program. Before library media specialists introduce specific changes, they should try to create an attitude of open-mindedness or acceptance of change among the faculty. As initiators of change, library media specialists can use humorous stories, jokes, cartoons, poems, and even videos to emphasize the need to look at what we are doing and why we are doing it. The video *The Calf Path*[18] from Phi Delta Kappa International does an excellent job of illustrating the sometimes foolish reasons for long-standing practices. Once teachers are willing to accept a change of any sort, they will be more willing to embrace those changes necessary for information literacy instruction.

Coordinating

Because library media specialists serve all teachers and all students, they are familiar with all the subject matter being taught. This familiarity makes library media specialists natural coordinators of the information literacy instruction program. As coordinators, they work with individual teachers or teams of teachers to develop thought-provoking units of study that include information literacy goals and objectives. These units are then taught cooperatively by the teachers and the library media specialists. Library media specialists become teachers as they instruct students (in entire classes, in small groups, or individually) in the research process and information-seeking strategies. They, like teachers, also should model information literacy skills when working with students. And they, as well as teachers, evaluate the development of skills, the research process, and the information product.

Aligning information literacy standards to local or state curriculum standards (similar to what has been done in appendixes A, B, C, D, and E) is helpful because it enables teachers to visualize the integration of both sets of standards and skills. The Checklist of Information Literacy Skills presented in chapter 8 is also a useful tool for instructional planning and record keeping.

Another task of the coordinator is to create an information-rich environment and to ensure that all teachers and students have access to the materials they need for authentic, resource-based learning experiences. Acquiring or finding appropriate information sources and notifying teachers of their availability are vital responsibilities of the coordinator of the information literacy instruction program.

SUMMARY

An effective school-wide information literacy program depends on an environment that fosters meaningful learning experiences full of opportunities for students to seek, evaluate, organize, and use information. The focus of these experiences is on understanding information in all its forms rather than on memorizing facts. In most schools this requires changes in the way the school day is organized, information is viewed, teachers teach, and students are evaluated. For lasting improvements, the entire school community must be involved both in the change process and in the everyday practices of an information literacy program. Principals, teachers, families, students, and library media specialists all have a part to play in fostering information literacy in the daily life of the school.

NOTES

1.   From *Teaching School: Points Picked Up*. Copyright © 1979, 1981 by Eric W. Johnson. Reprinted with permission from Walker and Company, 435 Hudson Street, New York, New York 10014. 1-800-289-2553. All Rights Reserved. Out of print. Described on the cover as "A book for anyone who is teaching, wants to teach, or knows a teacher," this book is full of helpful, practical ideas for teachers of all age levels—from discipline and organizing classrooms to tests and reporting to parents. Interesting and useful by itself, Johnson's book includes a valuable extra—*Points Picked Up: One Hundred Hints in How to Manage a School* by Abbie G. Hall, first published in 1891 by A. Flanigan. Some of the hints that fostered information literacy back in the 1800s are still relevant today. One example: "Every thing that is explained to a pupil which he can find out for himself robs him of so much education."

2.   Christine Susan Bruce, 1996, *Information Literacy Blueprint*. URL: http://www. gu.edu.au/ins/lils/infolit/blueprint/blueprnt.htm. (Accessed November 8, 1999). Reprinted by permission of Griffith University. This chart, in appendix 1, compares the Long Standing View of Learning to the Emerging View of Learning in seventeen different ways. It is taken from *Information Literacy—Challenging Roles for Information Professionals* by J. Kirk and R. Todd, 1993. Easily read, the chart offers a compact perspective on the changes occurring in education today.

3.   Reprinted with permission from National Science Education Standards. Copyright © 1995 by the National Academy of Sciences. Courtesy of the National Academy Press, Washington, DC. URL: http://www.nap.edu/readingroom/books/nses/html/index.html. (Accessed November 8, 1999). The "Changing Emphases" section lists nine methods or strategies that should be given less emphasis and corresponding items that should have more emphasis. One set suggests that less emphasis should be placed on "focusing on student acquisition of information," but more placed on "focusing on student understanding and use of scientific knowledge, ideas, and inquiry processes."

4.   Reprinted with permission from *Curriculum and Evaluation Standards for School Mathematics*, copyright 1989 by the National Council of Teachers of Mathematics. All rights reserved. The "Next Steps" section is also found on the Internet at URL: http://www.enc.org/reform/journals/enc2280/nf_280dtoc1.htm. A part of the Eisenhower National Clearinghouse Web site of the national mathematics standards, this section of the NCTM standards document contains explanations about the nature of change and change strategy and discusses specific reforms needed in the teaching of mathematics. The "Concluding Comments" include a vision of the new school mathematics program that expresses ideals for all school reforms.

5.   Debra Johnson and Cheryl L. Fox, 1998, *Critical Issue: Enhancing Learning Through Multiage Grouping*. URL: http://www.ncrel.org/sdrs/areas/issues/methods/ instrctn/in500.htm (Oakbrook, IL: North Central Regional Educational Laboratory, 1998). (Accessed November 8, 1999). Like other NCREL issues sites, this document gives an overview of the issue (multiage grouping), the goals, some action options, pitfalls and

different points of view, illustrative cases, and contacts for more information. There are links throughout to explanations of the terms used and other issues involved.

6. R. J. Dietal, J. L. Herman, and R. A. Knuth, 1991, *What Does Research Say About Assessment?* URL: http://www.ncrel.org/sdrs/areas/stw_esys/4assess.htm (Oakbrook, IL: North Central Regional Educational Laboratory, 1998). (Accessed November 8, 1999). Although focusing mainly on the pros and cons of standardized assessments, this article is valuable here for its purposes of assessment, characteristics of good assessment, and the common threads that link alternative assessments.

7. Tony Wagner, "Change as Collaborative Inquiry: A 'Constructivist' Methodology for Reinventing Schools," *Phi Delta Kappan* 79 (March 1998): 512–51. Used with permission. Tony Wagner is director of Consulting Services with Programs in Professional Education at Harvard Graduate School of Education. In this article, Mr. Wagner looks at educational reform from a constructivist point of view. The four stages of the change process and the old versus new viewpoints are 1) Defining the Problem: Failure Versus Obsolescence; 2) Developing Goals: Buy In Versus Ownership; 3) Implementation Strategies: Answers Versus Inquiry; and 4) Assessing Results: Summative Versus Formative. Concluding paragraphs discuss Leadership for Change: Dictating Versus Coaching and Compliance Versus Collaboration.

8. Daniel D. Barron, 1998, *Changing Paradigms*. URL: http://www.libsci.sc.edu/lisdec/telcon1/sld024.htm. (Accessed November 8, 1999). Derived from *Educating Jessica's Generation*, by Jostens Learning and reprinted by permission. The PowerPoint slides used in the AASL Information Literacy Teleconference are found on the Internet at http://www.libsci.sc.edu/lisdec/telcon1/index.htm. The teleconference was held on November 2, 1998, and was hosted by Dan Barron, Debbie Coleman Stone, and Martha Alewine. It gave historical background on the development of *Information Power: Building Partnerships for Learning* and offered implementation visions and directions.

9. Jan Buchanan, *Flexible Access Library Media Programs* (Englewood, CO: Libraries Unlimited, 1991). This book defines and describes a flexible access library media program, gives a justification for establishing a flexible access program, and provides suggestions on designing one. It also explains cooperative planning, and lists the roles and steps in implementing and evaluating a flexible access library media program.

10. Judy Harris Helm, 1997, *Active, Engaged, Meaningful Learning*. URL: http://www.ncrel.org/sdrs/areas/issues/students/earlycld/ea100.htm. (Oakbrook, IL: North Central Regional Educational Laboratory, 1998). (Accessed November 8, 1999). A link from the *Critical Issue: Organizing for Effective Early Childhood Programs and Practices*, this page explains the Piagetian theory behind active, engaged, meaningful learning for young students.

11. Kathy Checkley, "Homework—A New Look at an Age-Old Practice," *Education Update* 39 no. 7 (November 1997): 1, 5–6. Reprinted with permission from ASCD. All rights reserved. Checkley looks at homework through the recollections of several school

principals, then quotes their opinions of the characteristics of good, meaningful home-work assignments. The suggestions were that assignments should be realistic, should make allowances for all children, and should have a purpose that can be immediately defended.

12.   Robert L. DeBruyn, "The Reflection That Really Counts," *The MASTER Teacher* 30 (December 7, 1998). Reprinted by permission. Although the article addresses inter-personal behaviors, the same can be said of information-seeking behaviors. Passages that seem particularly relevant are "Without question, all subordinates learn from their superiors. . . . Indeed, they are observing and forming opinions and beliefs even when we don't see them looking. . . . Never think for a moment that your students don't learn from how you think and how you function. They learn from how you approach each day—as well as from how you approach work and handle problems. . . . The MASTER Teacher is well aware that little of what we do goes unnoticed. Students are constantly watching what we do and how we do it and why we do it."

13.   Home Committee of Community of Readers, 1998, *Twenty-Four Ideas for Parents and Children to Enjoy Reading in the Home* (unpublished document). This list of twenty-four strategies to encourage reading and learning it includes: *read aloud daily*; *search and research answers to questions together*; *start and maintain a home library of magazines, books, and newspapers*; and *read and talk about signs and labels in the home and community*. The other suggestions also are excellent, but these specifically foster in-formation literacy. A copy of this list is available from Charleston County School Dis-trict, 75 Calhoun Street, Charleston, SC 29401.

14.   Kent Brown, ed., *Highlights for Children* (Columbus, OH: Highlights for Chil-dren). This well-known magazine for children features stories, poems, and activities suit-able for young children.

15.   Cricket Magazine Group, *Cricket* (Peru, IL: Carus Publishing Company). One of several magazines for children published by the Cricket Magazine Group, this publica-tion is described and featured online at URL: http://www.cricketmag.com/cgi-bin/ cricket.cgi?tp/=home. The Web site offers interactive games as well as more informa-tion about the print magazine.

16.   *Cobblestone* (Peterborough, NH: Cobblestone Publishing). This magazine is for children ages seven to fourteen and contains articles on science, history, people, and cul-ture. It also is featured online at URL: http://www.cobblestonepub.com.

17.   Paula Montgomery, ed., *Crinkles* (Baltimore, MD: LMS Associates). From the publishers of *School Library Media Activities Monthly*, this magazine features articles and activities on topics of interest to children. It offers suggestions for further research and encourages children to explore the topics on their own.

18.   *The Calf Path*, Phi Delta Kappa International, 4 min. (Bloomington, IN: Phi Delta Kappa International), videocassette. This short, illustrated video is based on a poem by Sam Walter Foss. It tells the story of a calf path that wound through the woods and slowly

evolved into a winding major highway because no one thought of changing the way things had always been done. The poem challenges people not to always follow the "calf path of the mind" but to "chart new paths through our daily woods."

ADDITIONAL READINGS

Baker, Eve, ed. 1996. *Improving America's Schools: A Newsletter on Issues in School Reform.* URL: http://www.ed.gov/pubs/IASA/newsletters/assess/. Accessed November 8, 1999. This site focuses on the issue of student assessment and provides links to articles on creating better assessments, assessment requirements under Title I, and what the research says about student assessment.

Hydrick, Janie. *Parent's Guide to Literacy for the 21st Century: Pre–K Through Grade 5.* Urbana, IL: National Council of Teachers of English, 1996. This book explains to parents terms like "authentic assessment" that they may hear from teachers and other educators. It also contains activities that parents may do with children to promote a love of language and learning.

McKenzie, Jamieson. 1997. *The New "HomeWork."* URL: http://fno.org/feb97/teach.html. Accessed November 8, 1999. The subtitle, *Parents and Students Together on the Web: A Dozen Information Skills for the Home*, explains the contents of this site. It contains twelve activities to guide parents and their children in an exploration of the Internet.

Chapter **6**

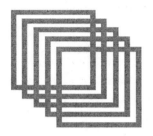

The Problem-Solving Component

The single best way to grow a better brain is through challenging problem solving.

—Eric Jensen

Growing better brains—teaching students to learn and think—is the business of educators. It is also the purpose of the whole information literacy movement. Information literacy instruction isn't limited to teaching students just how to learn; it includes teaching them how to think and solve problems, too. Because using information in critical thinking and problem solving (an indicator of information literacy) is a function of a better brain, teachers and library media specialists need to help students grow better brains by incorporating problem-solving instruction and activities into the daily curriculum of the school.

DEFINITION OF PROBLEM SOLVING

For some educators and many students the concept of problem solving includes pages of math problems or word problems at the end of a science chapter. A truer definition of problem solving involves every aspect of school and life. It is "the process of moving toward a goal when the path to that goal is uncertain."[1] If the path to the goal is clear, however difficult, the task is not a problem. The math or science "problems" that can be solved by using set procedures are not really problems, but exercises. These types of exercises help the brain become more efficient and the student more proficient, but they don't help the brain grow.[2]

The cognitive process of problem solving includes both critical- and creative-thinking skills. Critical thinking identifies the problem. Creative thinking brainstorms possible solutions. Critical thinking chooses the best of these. Creative thinking comes up with implementation ideas. Critical thinking then plans a practical strategy and evaluates the results. If the problem is not solved satisfactorily, creative thinking is employed again to produce alternative solutions or adaptations, and the cycle begins again.[3]

There are big problems and little problems, simple problems and more complex ones, but all true problem solving consists of trial and error, setbacks, and periods of uncertainty. Teachers and library media specialists need to remember the definition of problem solving and learn to tolerate the missteps and mistakes that will take place naturally during most problem-solving efforts.

IMPORTANCE OF PROBLEM SOLVING

Besides its value in growing better brains, are there other reasons for engaging students in problem-solving activities? Should teachers and library media specialists care whether or not students learn problem-solving skills? Is problem solving just another educational buzzword, or is it something that will benefit students for a lifetime? Is problem solving really that important? Employers, curriculum experts, and people who care about the future of the world seem to think so.

Workplace

According to a report titled *Building a Quality Workforce: Final Manuscript*, business leaders said they needed employees who could "identify problems, perceive alternative approaches and select the best approach."[4] In the government document *What Work Requires of Schools*, employers said they wanted workers to be competent in the following problem-solving skills:

- Creative Thinking—generates new ideas.

- Decision Making—specifies goals and constraints, generates alternatives, considers risks, and evaluates and chooses best alternative.

- Problem Solving—recognizes problems and devises and implements plan of action.

- Reasoning—discovers a rule or principle underlying the relationship between two or more objects and applies it in solving a problem.[5]

It is evident from these reports and others that the workplace needs employees who are skilled in critical thinking and problem solving. Students who leave school without these abilities will have difficulty finding and keeping meaningful jobs.

Educational Standards

Educators also see a need for students to learn problem-solving skills. All national curriculum standards include problem-solving objectives in their goals for student achievement, and all suggestions for school reform call for more problem-solving opportunities. Teachers and library media specialists who wish to follow national curriculum guidelines and engage all students in meaningful learning experiences should plan challenging problem-solving projects and activities for their pupils. The following sections highlight the problem-solving emphases of each of the national curriculum standards.

Math

The Curriculum and Evaluation Standards for School Mathematics contain five goals for students. One of these is for students to become mathematical problem solvers. Problem solving is described as "the process through which students discover and apply the power and utility of mathematics. Skill in problem solving is essential to productive citizenship."[6] The first standard, "Mathematics as Problem Solving," states that the study of mathematics should emphasize problem solving so that students can acquire confidence in using mathematics meaningfully. Applying mathematical skills to solve real-life problems provides a purpose for studying mathematics.

Science

The National Science Education Standards[7] address problem solving in content standards A and E. Content standard A states that students should understand and have the abilities to conduct scientific inquiries. These consist of asking questions, investigating, gathering data, and using that data to answer the questions; in other words—solving problems. Content standard E is even more specific. It says students should understand and have the abilities to implement technological design. This involves identifying a simple problem, proposing a solution, testing the solution, evaluating the product or design, and communicating the results. According to the standards, science teachers should provide students opportunities to participate both in scientific inquiry and in technological design.

English Language Arts

The ELA standards acknowledge the importance of problem solving by requiring students to use problem-solving skills in several situations. Standard 7 states that students will conduct research by posing problems. Even the research process itself, which is very similar to scientific inquiry, involves an information problem-solving procedure. Problem-solving skills also are needed for students to derive meaning from a variety of print or nonprint texts, to adjust the use of language to communicate effectively with a variety of audiences, and to apply knowledge of language to create print and nonprint information products.[8]

History

All the history standards require students to demonstrate their understanding of a concept by describing, comparing, analyzing, or creating a product such as a timeline, map, diary, chart, or narrative. Projects like these in which students have choices and decisions to make require problem-solving skills. The standards also promote the importance of problem solving by having students identify the historical problems of past generations and geographical locations, analyze the way these were addressed or solved, and determine the immediate and long-lasting effects of those solutions.[9]

Fine Arts

The fine arts standards support the importance of problem solving in each of the separate disciplines. Music, dance, visual arts, and drama all require students to apply appropriate criteria or techniques to communicate a particular message to a specific audience. For example, in interpretive dance, students are faced with the problem of depicting situations or emotions through movement. Determining what to do and how to do it involves a number of problem-solving skills.[10]

Thinking Skills

Problem solving is considered a higher-order thinking skill and is valuable in both professional and personal situations. According to the Learning Research and Development Center, higher-order thinking skills include the abilities to

- Size up and define a problem that isn't neatly packaged.

- Determine which facts and formulas stored in memory might be helpful for solving a problem.

- Recognize when more information is needed, and where and how to look for it.

- Deal with uncertainty by "brainstorming" possible ideas or solutions when the way to proceed isn't apparent.

- Carry out complex analyses or tasks that require planning, management, monitoring, and adjustment.

- Exercise judgment in situations where there aren't clear-cut "right" and "wrong" answers, but more and less useful ways of doing things.

- Step outside the routine to deal with an unexpected breakdown or opportunity.[11]

The latest research indicates that all students, especially at-risk students, benefit from instruction in higher-order thinking skills.[12] Problem-solving activities should not be reserved for gifted and talented students, but should be presented to everyone. Cooperative learning problem-solving exercises take advantage of the abilities of the best students while providing all children with opportunities to contribute ideas and information.

CONNECTION TO INFORMATION LITERACY

As stated previously, problem solving is a basic information literacy skill. The third AASL/AECT standard for student learning states that information-literate students "use information effectively and creatively." This means that in addition to organizing information and integrating it with their own knowledge, students also apply information in critical thinking and problem solving. Finding, accessing, evaluating, and even organizing information are only partially valuable skills by themselves. Students (and all people) have to be able to think about the information they have gathered, and use it to solve problems, make decisions, and improve their lives. Information by itself is inert. Only when it is used in thinking about decisions or problems does it become powerful and dynamic. If students understand the connection between information, thinking skills, and problem solving, learning becomes more meaningful and students become more information literate.

FOSTERING PROBLEM-SOLVING ABILITIES

The process of problem solving involves thinking skills. Unfortunately though, according to Barry Beyer, professor of education emeritus at George Mason University, "Everyone thinks. But very few of us think as well as we should."[13] That is the purpose of education—and specifically information literacy instruction: to create better learners, thinkers, and problem solvers. Because good thinking doesn't happen by happy accident,[14] teachers and library media specialists must deliberately foster thinking and problem-solving abilities by creating proper classroom environments, teaching helpful techniques, modeling good thinking behaviors, and providing ample opportunities for problem-solving experiences.

Classroom Environment

By definition, problem solving is an uncertain journey. Students who engage in problem-solving activities understandably make mistakes. A classroom atmosphere that tolerates mistakes and does not condone ridicule by peers allows students to relax and think freely without fear of embarrassment. Young children are natural problem solvers who are not afraid of making mistakes; for them, life is one series of problems after another and tackling them is an all-consuming challenge.[15] Only when children grow older and are mocked for saying the wrong thing or for doing something in an unconventional way do they become scared of taking risks and making mistakes. Most older students tackle problem solving with anxiety because of their fear of failure or of not finding the right answer. If elementary teachers maintain an atmosphere of acceptance, where all ideas are considered with respect and occasional mistakes are expected, students may retain their natural problem-solving tendencies.

Teaching Techniques

Although the path to the goal is unclear, problem solving is not a completely mysterious, hit-or-miss process. Various techniques or strategies can be employed to facilitate solving all types of problems. The first, most obvious strategy is to ask, "Have I seen or heard about this type of problem before? Have I or someone else solved this problem before? Will that solution, or some adaptation of it, work with this problem?" Teachers and library media specialists should guide students to ask themselves these questions and to look for patterns or similarities in problems. This process not only helps them find solutions to the immediate problems but also helps them become aware that patterns or similarities in problems exist. This knowledge aids in the transfer of problem-solving skills to other academic or personal dilemmas.

Some other techniques that teachers and students can use are called heuristics and are the general "rules of thumb" of problem solving.[16] One distinguishing attribute of a heuristic is its unpredictability. Using a particular heuristic may help a student solve a problem, but it may not, either. Success is not guaranteed. Several heuristics are explained and illustrated below.[17] Teachers and library media specialists must model, teach, and discuss these techniques with their students to foster good thinking and problem-solving abilities.

Means-Ends Analysis

Many times a problem seems too big; the goal appears too distant. It is so overwhelming, students don't know where to begin. The means-ends analysis technique breaks the problem into smaller parts, each a subset of the overall goal. Students work on one subgoal at a time, slowly progressing a little closer to the final goal with each step. Mistakes and setbacks are expected, but each success increases the students' confidence about eventually solving the problem. If students complain that a problem is too complicated to solve, encourage them to take the first step and do just one thing that will get them closer to the goal. Often the first step is the most important.

Mr. Allen gave each student a mass of tangled yarn. "This is your problem," he said. "How will you solve it? How will you untangle the yarn?" As the students began to pull ends through holes and untie knots, he pointed out that each move got them a little closer to their goal. They couldn't untangle the yarn in one step, he explained, but if they worked on it bit by bit, one little section at a time, eventually it would all come free.

When all the yarn was untangled, Mr. Allen and his students brainstormed about other problems that could be tackled in this manner: memorizing the multiplication tables, researching a topic, developing a multimedia project, working through a complicated math problem, playing a checkers game, studying a social studies chapter, conducting a campaign for a community playground, and many more.

Working Backwards

Occasionally, the goal is the only clear part of a problem. With this technique, students start with the goal and think what should happen one step before the goal. Then they consider what should be right before that. Working backwards this way, students eventually arrive at the first step in the process. Once this first step is known, students can work forwards to complete the problem.

Ms. Clark's students said they wanted a flower garden. "Great!" she replied. "Let's think . . . what must we do to have flowers?" As the students thought backwards, they realized that before they could have flowers, they needed to plant seeds or bulbs. Before that, they would need to prepare the soil and test it for nutrients, and before that they would have to collect the necessary gardening tools and decide on the best place to put the flower garden. Working backwards, they decided that first they must ask the principal for permission to have a flower garden; next, they must gather information about what kinds of flowers grow best in different locations.

Successive Approximation

Anyone who has written a rough draft, then added, deleted, edited, and revised, has engaged in successive approximation. The goal is eventually reached, but only after numerous revisions, adaptations, modifications, and improvements.

Many creative works are approached in this manner—paintings, musical scores, Web pages, recipes, inventions, and even theories. The knowledge that experts use this process gives students the encouragement to continue improving on a project or product until it meets their standards.

> *Mrs. McDuffie's class had to write and produce a play for the February PTSA meeting. After brainstorming ideas, they decided to do something about Harriet Tubman and the Underground Railroad in honor of Black History Month. After several weeks of writing and revising the script, one student suggested they include some appropriate music and songs. These improvements were incorporated into the play. Then someone else suggested they add African dances and still another suggested a narrator. On it went as the play progressed from a single idea to a finished production.*

External Representation

Students can use external representation to get a clearer picture of the problem or to portray it to someone else. When a problem contains too many parts to think of at once, or the relationships between the parts are complicated, it may be helpful to draw a picture, make a list, create a chart, draw a diagram, or otherwise depict the problem visually. Often, just seeing the problem on paper makes the problem-solving process easier. Sometimes, someone else can view the problem and immediately see a solution. External representation is a good strategy to use for group problem-solving activities.

> *Ms. Clark's students thought they were ready to plant the seeds and bulbs for their flower garden. They had received permission from the principal, picked a suitable location, decided on the particular flowers they wanted, gathered tools and plantings, and were excited about getting to work. But as they began bickering about the tools, the plantings, and the space, they realized they had some more problems to work out. Back in the classroom, they drew an outline of the garden on the board. Using colored chalk, they plotted locations for the flowers, then assigned groups of students to each area. Drawing a picture of the garden helped the students arrange the flowers aesthetically and divide the work fairly.*

Good Thinking Behaviors

Because good thinking does not always come naturally, teachers and library media specialists need to accept the responsibility for teaching and modeling good thinking strategies and behaviors. Even elementary educators can discuss these attitudes with their students.

The following behaviors are taken from "The Vital Strategies of Skilled Thinkers," published in *The MASTER Teacher*.[18] "Effective thinkers take their time." Thinkers who take their time don't run the risk of jumping to conclusions or grabbing at the first answer or solution that comes to mind. Deliberate thinking takes time to consider all sides of the question. Teachers who recognize this allow students time to answer questions or work on problems. They do not always call on the student who has the quickest answer.

"Skilled thinkers are purposeful and intentional in their thinking—and focus their attention on a particular purpose or situation." These thinkers stick to their topics. Knowing clearly what it is they wish to accomplish with their thinking, they set their minds on a goal and work continuously toward it, considering all information or ideas that may help them along the way.

"Skilled thinkers discipline themselves to remain objective." Good thinkers do not allow their thinking to be influenced by personal feelings. They keep an open mind until they have considered all possible solutions and the pros and cons of each of these. They do not make a decision or consider a problem solved until all alternatives have been examined equally.

"Skilled thinkers avoid the either/or trap." When faced with a dilemma, good thinkers go beyond the first two choices that come to mind—which are usually opposites. They realize that often the best solutions are not obvious at first. Consequently, they force themselves to consider additional alternatives and to look at the problem creatively from different perspectives before making a decision.

"Skilled thinkers develop effective listening and observation skills." Good thinkers are aware of their surroundings and are cognizant of the opportunities they offer for learning. These people are constantly gathering information on any number of subjects by listening and observing. These bits of information are stored in the brain and brought forth later when a need arises. When faced with a problem or a decision, good thinkers consider what they have learned and how it can help them. Have they, or someone they know, encountered this situation before? What was the solution then? Will it fit this time?

"Skilled thinkers allow themselves to be curious." Good thinkers ask questions and get involved in interesting things without worrying about appearing foolish. By asking questions, they add to the knowledge gathered through listening and observing. They learn to recognize patterns in problems or situations; they use what they have learned from past experiences (their own and others') to develop solutions. They realize that a broad and varied foundation of knowledge helps solve problems and information needs.

Problem-Based Learning

Problem solving, like all other information literacy skills, should not be taught in isolation. For students to transfer problem-solving skills to everyday life, they should be involved in solving realistic, everyday problems. Authentic problem-solving activities give purpose to the content that students must master for each discipline. They answer the age-old question, "Why do we need to learn this?" by vividly demonstrating the value of information in real-life situations.

How do teachers and library media specialists think of ideas for appropriate problem-solving activities? Remembering the definition of problem solving makes the process easier. Any project or activity that is not dictated by the teacher but that requires trial and error or decision making by the student (the path to the goal is uncertain) involves problem solving. All problem solving is valuable, whether it is as simple as figuring out how to center text on a computer or as complicated as designing an entire Web site. When students are engaged in the process, they are growing better brains.

Many times instructional units can be converted to problem-solving projects. In these instances, national, state, or local curriculum standards are good starting points. During the planning process, teachers and library media specialists can analyze the content standards by asking themselves several questions: "Who would need this type of information?" "What kinds of jobs or hobbies depend on knowledge like this?" "In what situations would it be useful?" Then, working backwards, "Do any of these situations relate to my students?" "What sorts of problems might my students encounter that could be solved by this information?" Discovering a problem that affects students personally helps by motivating students and enhancing the learning experience.

Whenever possible, take advantage of current events or community issues when planning problem-solving units. Older students may even be able to do some original research and make valuable contributions by sharing their findings with the experts who are working on the problem. Students who see the impact of their learning on their lives and the lives of others realize the power of information when it is used in critical thinking and problem solving.

SUMMARY

The ability to apply information in critical thinking and problem solving is one of the major characteristics of an information-literate person. Because this skill is considered crucial by employers and educators, teachers and library media specialists have the responsibility to teach students how to think and how to solve problems. Fortunately, according to experts, one way of helping students to think is to offer opportunities for challenging problem solving. This presents an exciting cycle of opportunities—challenging problem-solving activities create competent problem solvers.

NOTES

1.   Michael E. Martinez, "What Is Problem Solving?" *Phi Delta Kappan* 79 (April 1998): 605–9. Reprinted by permission. This article discusses problem solving, the importance of teaching it, classroom conditions that encourage problem solving, and some techniques or strategies that can be taught to help students solve problems. The author stresses that "by its nature, problem solving involves error and uncertainty." He states that young children are natural problem solvers and schools should encourage this ability by tolerating occasional mistakes and asking for a variety of possible answers rather than requiring one right answer and punishing all wrong ones.

2.   From *Teaching with the Brain in Mind* by Eric Jensen. Alexandria, VA: Association for Supervision and Curriculum Development. Copyright © 1998 ASCD. Reprinted by permission. All rights reserved. Jensen explains some of the latest research on the brain and how factors such as threats, stress, motivation, rewards, emotions, and movement affect the brain and learning. He describes an enriched environment that contributes to brain development as one that is challenging and provides interactive feedback. Each chapter offers practical suggestions or strategies for incorporating what we know about the workings of the brain into classroom activities. Jensen states, "To our brain, we are either doing something we already know how to do or we are doing something new. If we are repeating an earlier learning, there's a good chance the neural pathways will become more and more efficient. . . . While exercise is doing what we already know how to do, stimulation is doing something new. . . . As long as it's coherent, this novel mental or motor stimulation produces greater beneficial electrical energy than the old-hat stuff."

3.   John Chaffee, *Thinking Critically*, 2d ed. Copyright © 1988 by Houghton Mifflin Company. In his book, Chaffee, director of the Center for Critical Thinking and Language Learning at the City University of New York, explains the relationship between critical and creative thinking and problem solving. Chaffee believes that "thinking is an ability that can be developed and improved through guidance and practice" and that good thinking habits are necessary for good decision making and successful problem solving.

4.   Glen Thomas and Gaye Smoot, "Critical Thinking: A Vital Work Skill," *Trust for Educational Leadership* 23 (February/March 1994): 34–38. Reprinted with permission from *Trust for Educational Leadership*. This article also can be viewed on the Internet at http://www.enc.org/reform/journals/enc2315/2315.htm. The authors cite several sources that state the need for students to learn critical-thinking skills in school. They also recognize that some parents and even some teachers may be opposed to the idea. In addition to stressing the importance of critical thinking, the authors explain the controversy surrounding it, and offer helpful ideas for handling the conflict. When discussing critical thinking, they state that students "need to be able to apply the knowledge learned in one setting to new situations in their daily life at work and at home. Critical thinking is not an activity that is done later, after a series of skills are mastered, nor is it reserved for only the very brightest students. Rather, all students must think critically as they encounter new information in order to understand what it means and why it is significant."

5.   Secretary's Commission on Achieving Necessary Skills, *What Work Requires of Schools: A SCANS Report for America 2000* (Washington, DC: U.S. Government Printing Office, 1991). The complete list of thinking skills is included in the SCANS section of chapter 2. The "Notes" and "Additional Readings" sections of that chapter contain annotated citations.

6.   Reprinted by permission from *Curriculum and Evaluation Standards for School Mathematics.* Copyright 1989 by the National Council of Teachers of Mathematics. All rights reserved. The standards can be found on the Internet at URL: http://www.enc.org/reform/journals/enc2280/nf_280dtoc1.htm. Cited previously in chapter 3, the math standards stress problem-solving skills in Standard 1: Mathematics as Problem Solving. The specific skills are listed in appendix A.

7.   Reprinted with permission from *National Science Education Standards.* Copyright © 1995 by the National Academy of Sciences. Courtesy of the National Academy Press, Washington, DC. URL: http://www.nap.edu/readingroom/books/nses/html/index.html. (Accessed November 8, 1999). An annotated citation for this site can be found in chapter 3.

8.   *Standards for the English Language Arts* by the International Reading Association and National Council of Teachers of English. Copyright 1996 by the International Reading Association and the National Council of Teachers of English. Reprinted by permission. (Urbana, IL: NCTE, 1996). A copy of the twelve standards can be found on the Internet at http://www.didaxinc.com/standards/langstandards.html. An annotated citation is included in the "Notes" section of chapter 3.

9.   National Center for History in the Schools, *National Standards for Grades K–4 History* (Los Angeles: National Center for History in the Schools, 1995). By permission of the National Center for History in the Schools at UCLA. An annotation for the history standards is in chapter 3. The standards themselves are shown in appendix C.

10.   National Consortium for Arts Education, *National Standards for Arts Education* (Reston, VA: Music Educators National Conference, 1994). See annotation for the arts standards in chapter 3. The standards themselves are shown in appendix E.

11.   Learning Research and Development Center, University of Pittsburgh, *The New Standards Project: An Overview* (Pittsburgh, PA: Learning Research and Development Center, 1991). This resource was mentioned in a NCREL Web site on thinking skills. The thinking skills page is a link from the At-Risk Students issues site.

12.   Karen Rasmussen, "Liberating Minds: Helping Students Take Charge of Their Thinking," *Education Update* 40 (August 1998): 1, 4–5. Used with permission from ASCD. All rights reserved. In this article, Rasmussen discusses the abandonment of "pour and store" educational practices in favor of teaching students how to think. She stresses that thinking skills should be taught to all students through content areas and with special emphasis on how thinking skills can be transferred to real-life situations.

Rasmussen says students should be encouraged to take charge of their own thinking through reflection and self-evaluation.

13. Ibid. Rasmussen quotes Barry Beyer in explaining why teachers are working to help students acquire thinking skills and take charge of their own thinking. The complete quote reads, "We're not trying to teach people to think. Everyone thinks. But very few of us think as well as we should when we deal with the complex issues we face as voters and consumers."

14. Ibid. This statement is part of the following quote from Barry Beyer: "A lot of people believe that good thinking happens by happy accident—if you put kids in a rich environment, their thinking will improve. It doesn't work that way for most kids."

15. Martinez. The author states that problem solving isn't just for older learners, and young children are the most natural problem solvers.

16. Ibid. Martinez distinguishes between general heuristics ("usually content free and apply across many different situations") and specific heuristics ("used in specialized areas, often specific subject domains or professions"). This chapter on problem solving deals with general heuristics only.

17. Ibid. These explanations of the four heuristics listed (means-ends analysis, working backward, successive approximation, and external representation) come from the article, "What Is Problem Solving?"

18. Robert L. DeBruyn, "The Vital Strategies of Skilled Thinkers," *The MASTER Teacher* 30 (November 9, 1998). Reprinted by permission. This article outlines six behaviors of skilled thinkers and urges teachers to "invite students to share their thinking processes aloud."

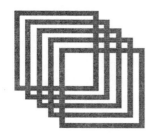

Chapter **7**

Creating All the Parts

All men by nature desire knowledge.
—Aristotle

We are an intelligent species and the use of our intelligence quite properly gives us pleasure. In this respect the brain is like a muscle. When it is in use we feel very good. Understanding is joyous.
—Carl Sagan

Aristotle speaks a truth. Carl Sagan explains why this is true. If some of today's students don't appear joyous about learning, perhaps it is because educators are not teaching them in ways they can understand. Not all students learn when taught through traditional methods. Therefore, they never experience the joyous feelings of understanding. If educators hope to reach each child, to create a love of learning and instill good thinking skills and attitudes, i.e., to foster information literacy, then they need to take advantage of all the recent research about brain development, learning styles, multiple intelligences, and thinking skills in order to design learning experiences that address the needs of every student.

The Learning Design Model[1] (see figure 7.1) graphically depicts the issues that must be considered when designing learning experiences, and shows how all the pieces are related. The process described takes into account all the elements necessary to fulfill the information needs of a specific group of learners to reach differing intelligences, personalities, and learning styles, and to address all levels of learning. This chapter focuses on three of these issues: designing learning experiences to meet the needs of the students and the curriculum, understanding differences in learners, and teaching thinking skills that are vital to information literacy growth.

FOCUSING ON DESIGN

Teachers and library media specialists are responsible for working together to design units or lessons that fulfill both curriculum and information literacy goals and objectives. Teachers are experts on matters concerning the academic curriculum and individual student learning styles and abilities; library media specialists are experts on information literacy instruction, information resources, and related technologies. Together they collaborate on designing lessons that meet curriculum standards and information literacy objectives and that engage all students in hands-on, challenging, real-life problem-solving activities.

Collaborating

Collaboration between teachers and library media specialists is accomplished through a combination of scheduled planning sessions, memos, quick conferences in the hallway, and even e-mail messages. Scheduled sessions are most effective for major planning, but memos or e-mail messages are helpful in the beginning and for minor clarifications.

Many library media specialists send monthly memos to teachers requesting information about upcoming curriculum topics or themes (see figure 7.2, page 95). Armed with this knowledge, the library media specialist checks available resources, secures additional sources if necessary, and becomes familiar with the topic. Then, in the planning session, the professionals brainstorm, discuss, and lay out the activities of the unit. In particular, they plan how the unit will be introduced, which information literacy skills will be focused on, how they will be taught, what activities will be used to guide students' research into the topic, what types of information products will be created, and how these will be evaluated. They also specify the responsibilities of all involved.

Sometimes the collaboration is between one self-contained classroom teacher and the library media specialist, and possibly at least one exploratory teacher. Occasionally, an entire grade level will study the same topic or theme and all those teachers will meet with the library media specialist for a joint planning session. At other times, two or more subject-area teachers confer with the library media specialist to plan interdisciplinary units of study. There are pros and cons

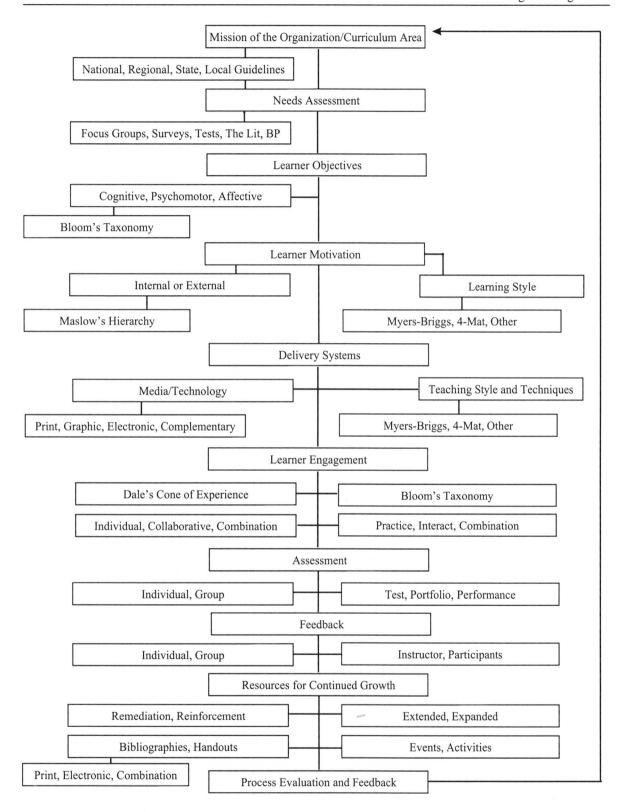

Fig. 7.1. Learning Design Model. Developed by Daniel D. Barron. Used with permission.

concerning total grade-level participation in studying one thematic unit. On the plus side, thematic units are great unifying forces that create an *esprit de corps* and offer opportunities for grade-level celebrations and culminating activities. On the negative side, whole-grade participation means the information resources will be divided among many more students. Teachers and library media specialists should consider these pros and cons during the planning process.

Figure 7.3 (see pages 96–97) is a lesson plan model that lists the points to be discussed and decided upon in the planning sessions. The planning guide (see figure 7.2) and a lesson plan outline (similar to that of figure 7.3) are included on the disk that came with this book. Teachers and library media specialists are encouraged to use these tools when planning and designing lessons, units, or other learning experiences.

Considering Styles and Skills

During the planning stage, teachers and library media specialists also consider the different learning styles and abilities of their students. Providing a number of resources in a variety of formats ensures that every student will be able to access and comprehend information from at least some of the sources. Permitting choices in presentation formats allows students to use their individual talents to create information products. Both practices increase the opportunities for success for all students. Differences between students and their impact on learning are discussed later in this chapter.

Another issue to be considered during the lesson design phase is the incorporation of critical-thinking skills. Teachers and library media specialists must decide on the level of difficulty desired, how the skills will be taught, the tools that can help (charts, webs, etc.), and how students will be assessed. This stage of the planning process is often overlooked, but critical-thinking and problem-solving skills, like other information literacy skills, are too important to be left to chance. Critical-thinking skills are discussed in depth later in this chapter.

Adding Layers

It may be beneficial to compare the designing of a unit or lesson to the process of adding on layers. The bottom layer, or foundation, consists of the unit topic (or theme) and the goals and objectives (both curriculum and information literacy). Usually teachers are responsible for the topic and the curriculum goals and objectives. Library media specialists decide which information literacy objectives relate, or which skills are needed. These must be determined before any other planning can be accomplished.

The next layer to be added (or issue to be considered) concerns the information sources. What resources are available? Which ones are appropriate for this group? Are there enough? Are more needed? This stage should be completed early in the process so additional resources may be secured if necessary.

PLANNING GUIDE

Teacher(s)

Grade

Topic or Unit Theme

Dates of Unit

Resources Needed

Activities Planned

Types of Projects or Products

Number/Type(s) of Sources Required

Special Considerations?

Fig. 7.2. Planning Guide.

LESSON PLAN MODEL

The following is the framework of a lesson plan that integrates information literacy skills with curriculum (subject-area) skills. The model may be used to outline a single lesson or a unit of study. It should be developed jointly by the classroom teacher and the library media specialist, with special attention given to the responsibilities of both. This model is adapted from the outline followed by *School Library Media Activities Monthly* and is used with permission from LMS Associates.

LESSON TITLE

GRADE LEVEL

NEEDS ASSESSMENT

The needs assessment should be based on the national, state, and district standards or guidelines for the particular subject area, the AASL/AECT Information Literacy Standards, and an assessment of students' strengths and weaknesses in information literacy skills.

CURRICULUM (SUBJECT-AREA) GOALS

Subject-area goals are broad, general expectations that are derived from curriculum standards or frameworks. "Students will…"

CURRICULUM (SUBJECT-AREA) OBJECTIVES

Subject-area objectives are specific, measurable expectations derived from curriculum standards or frameworks. "The student will be able to…"

INFORMATION LITERACY GOALS

Information literacy goals are broad, general expectations that are derived from the *Information Literacy Standards for Student Learning.* "Students will…"

INFORMATION LITERACY OBJECTIVES

Information literacy objectives are specific, measurable expectations derived from the indicators in *the Information Literacy Standards for Student Learning.* "The student will be able to…"

RESPONSIBILITIES OF THE SUBJECT-AREA TEACHER(S)

These responsibilities will include, but will not be limited to, introducing, explaining, and overseeing any activities conducted in the classroom; assisting students in the research process; and evaluating the product and the process.

RESPONSIBILITIES OF THE LIBRARY MEDIA SPECIALIST

These responsibilities will include, but will not be limited to, obtaining any necessary resources; providing instruction in information literacy skills; assisting students in the research process; and participating in the evaluation process.

RESOURCES

Resources may include print (books, periodicals, pamphlets, etc.), nonprint (filmstrips, videos, ITV/ETV programs, CD-ROMs, the Internet, etc.), or knowledgeable people. A variety of resources facilitates understanding by students with different learning styles.

ACTIVITIES

All activities of the lesson or unit should be listed and assigned to either the classroom teacher or the library media specialist. Authentic, challenging, problem-solving activities foster motivation and encourage transfer of skills to everyday life.

EVALUATION

A rubric, which clearly states the requirements of an excellent, adequate, or inadequate project, is a valuable evaluation tool.

Both the research process and the end product need to be evaluated.

FOLLOW-UP ACTIVITES

Follow-up activities are intended to reinforce student learning, extend student interest, and provide opportunities for discussion. Some of the follow-up activities may be mandated by the evaluation results.

Fig. 7.3. Lesson Plan Model.

LESSON PLAN MODEL

LESSON TITLE

GRADE LEVEL

TEACHER(S)

NEEDS ASSESSMENT

CURRICULUM (SUBJECT-AREA) GOALS

CURRICULUM (SUBJECT-AREA) OBJECTIVES

INFORMATION LITERACY GOALS

INFORMATION LITERACY OBJECTIVES

RESPONSIBILITIES OF THE SUBJECT-AREA TEACHER(S)

RESPONSIBILITIES OF THE LIBRARY MEDIA SPECIALIST

RESOURCES

ACTIVITIES

EVALUATION

FOLLOW-UP ACTIVITES

Fig. 7.4. Blank Lesson Plan Model.

Another layer consists of the major activities and projects. What problems will the students solve? How will they get their information? What will they create to demonstrate their learning? When this layer is completed, the entire plan is considered again and examined for methods to address different learning styles and talents. Will all students have an opportunity for success?

Finally, the unit is given one last analysis—one last layer. This time the focus is on higher-order thinking skills and transfer of learning. Are the students really being challenged to *think* (to *use* information) and not just to repeat what they have read or heard? Are the skills being taught transferable to other subject areas or life situations? Is the learning meaningful and worthwhile? If the answer to the last question is "Yes," and all other questions are answered satisfactorily, then the final layer has been added and the design process is complete.

Designing As Problem Solving

Planning an interdisciplinary thematic unit or lesson is much like any problem-solving activity—the path to the goal is unclear. Many times the goal—the curriculum goal—is the only clear part of the problem. Teachers and library media specialists work backwards to determine what activities will accomplish the goal, what skills are necessary, what problems can be solved, what resources will be needed, etc. Often, the unit is broken into parts as the teachers and library media specialists tackle one segment at a time (first the topic, then the activities, then the skills, etc.) until the problem of the unit plan is solved. Sometimes teachers and library media specialists depict the unit graphically, using different shapes and colors to represent the different subject areas, objectives, and thinking skills. This technique shows at a glance which areas are covered and which ones need to be addressed. Finally, as with all creative works, the unit plan is revised, added to, adjusted, and improved as teachers and library media specialists move forward on an uncertain course. Mistakes are normal—an occasional lesson flop is expected—but failures are minimized if all issues are considered in the unit design process.

FOCUSING
ON THE LEARNER

Students are different. They look and act differently. They have different personalities, learning styles, talents, interests, and abilities. They come from different cultural backgrounds and family lifestyles. They have different needs and wants and priorities. They are individuals. The best way to reach all students is to accept them as individuals—to acknowledge their differences and plan for them when creating and designing learning experiences.

Different Needs

Some students come to school ready to learn. They have enough sleep, enough food, enough clothing, and enough attention and love to feel safe, confident, and eager to learn. Unfortunately, other students come to school without enough sleep, food, clothing, attention, or love. According to Abraham Maslow's Hierarchy of Needs,[2] until these students' basic physiological and safety needs are met, they will have difficulty focusing on anything academic or school-related. Although these are primarily parents' responsibilities, schools and communities try to compensate for the differences in parental support so that all students will be able to learn.

Students also need to feel accepted and appreciated before they can learn. While classroom teachers and library media specialists are not personally responsible for feeding and clothing those students who do not have enough, they are responsible for creating an atmosphere of acceptance. This means welcoming students, accepting their ideas and contributions, and even tolerating their occasional mistakes. It also means treating students with respect and dignity, even when disciplining them. Threats, ridicule, and sarcasm are counterproductive to learning. The reactions of students to the stress of an unfriendly classroom are not only emotional but physical as well. Stress actually causes the brain to shut down—students get confused about what is important and what is not, they have difficulty distinguishing patterns, and they have trouble remembering. In fact, according to one educator, "excess stress and threat in the school environment may be the single greatest contributor to impaired academic learning."[3] If teachers and library media specialists want to create environments conducive to learning, they must keep in mind the basic needs of all students and the individual needs of each.

Different Intelligences

Differences between students are even more apparent in their talents, abilities, and intelligences. Howard Gardner's research and theory of multiple intelligences suggests that people have different ways of thinking, expressing ideas, and solving problems.[4] He identifies eight distinct abilities or ways of thinking: linguistic, logical-mathematical, spatial, musical, bodily-kinesthetic, interpersonal, intrapersonal, and naturalist. Although all students possess each of these intelligences in varying degrees, many students have some that are more highly developed than others.

Students who have linguistic intelligence think in words and are talented in using language to express ideas. Students who have logical-mathematical intelligence like numbers and puzzles and are talented in solving problems logically. Spatially intelligent students think in pictures and can create images and designs. Musically intelligent students can distinguish pitch, rhythm, and tone and can use music expressively. Students who have bodily-kinesthetic intelligence like using their hands and bodies to express ideas and emotions. Interpersonal intelligence means students understand and interact well with other people. Intrapersonal intelligence means students understand themselves.[5] Gardner's latest discovery, naturalist intelligence, is the ability some students have to "recognize plants, animals, and other parts of the natural environment, like clouds or rocks." This kind of intelligence also relates to recognizing man-made objects like cars, sneakers, and jewelry.[6]

When asked what message he would like to send concerning multiple intelligences and the classroom, Gardner encourages teachers to "pay attention to the differences among kids and try to use that knowledge to personalize instruction and assessment." He also cautions against labeling students as "being" one thing and not another, stating that "the intelligences are categories that help us discover differences in forms of mental representation; they are not good characterizations of what people are (or are not) like."[7]

Different Learning Styles

Not all students think in the same way; similarly, not all students learn in the same manner. Different students have different learning styles that sometimes determine success or failure in school. Teachers and library media specialists have particular teaching styles that are related to their own learning styles. Students whose learning styles are compatible with the teachers' teaching styles are successful. Others are less so.

Teachers and library media specialists who wish to provide meaningful learning experiences for all students need to monitor their own teaching styles, pay attention to the different learning styles represented in their classrooms, and discuss these with their colleagues. The difficulty lies in the fact that there are almost as many ways to describe learning styles as there are different ways of learning.[8] Terms like *visual, kinesthetic,* and *auditory,*[9] expressions like *Show and Tellers* and *Leaders of the Pack,*[10] and descriptions of Type 1 (Innovative) Learners and Type 3 (Common Sense) Learners[11] all portray various ways of perceiving, processing, and responding to information. The important concept for teachers and library media specialists to remember is that there are differences and to plan for these in designing learning experiences.

How do teachers determine their students' learning styles? Elementary teachers observe students carefully to determine how they learn best. *Does Susie catch on better when she reads the information, or when it is told to her? Does Johnny work better in groups or by himself? Is Billy always asking why he has to learn something new, or does he pursue ideas on his own?*

Also, teachers or library media specialists may determine students' styles by administering learning style surveys or inventories. The *Dunn and Dunn Learning Styles Inventory,* used by many schools to assess students' learning styles, considers twenty-two environmental, emotional, sociological, physical, or psychological preferences.[12] Another learning style survey, featured in *Running a School Library Media Center,*[13] was designed by the Murdock Teacher Center in

Wichita, Kansas. In it, students respond to statements such as "I remember what I have read better than what I've heard" with degrees of "Most Like Me" or "Least Like Me." These are the different learning styles identified by the developers of this survey:

1. *Auditory linguistic*: prefers to learn by means of spoken word.

2. *Visual linguistic*: prefers to see words in order to learn.

3. *Auditory numerical*: learns easily from hearing numbers and oral explanations.

4. *Visual numerical*: prefers to see numbers in order to learn.

5. *Audiovisual-kinesthetic combination*: likes a combination of the three basic modalities.

6. *Individual learner*: works best alone.

7. *Group learner*: likes learning with others.

8. *Oral expressive*: prefers to share knowledge by telling others.

9. *Written expressive*: prefers to share knowledge by writing.[14]

As suggested previously, teachers should be aware of students' particular learning styles, but that does not mean students should be taught only in that method. Most educators agree that a mixture of teaching styles is best for all learners. In fact, some experts believe that ideas should be introduced in the manner students learn best, but for deeper learning and understanding, ideas should be examined in other ways as well.[15]

Bernice McCarthy, developer of the 4-MAT® System[16] framework for instructional design, suggests that teachers, not students, take a learning styles survey. McCarthy co-wrote the Learning Type Measure (LTM), which is a self-report assessment for adults. This assessment enables teachers to identify their own individual preferences for approaching the world of experience. According to McCarthy, when teachers or students are engaged in new learning, two dimensions must be taken into account: The first dimension is how they perceive new learning; the second is how they process or internalize their learning experiences.

The 4-MAT® System recognizes that the perception continuum ranges from those who initially take in new experiences through sensing and feeling to those who make their initial appraisals of learning through their intellects by thinking. Neither dimension is better than the other. Some people "sense and feel" first, while others "think" first. After learners take in new experiences, they must process the experiences to internalize them and make them their own. This processing dimension suggests a second continuum. Some people process initially by reflecting on new experiences, while others process first by acting. Again, neither way of processing is better than the other. It is simply what works best for each individual learner.

McCarthy contends that when these two dimensions of perceiving and processing are juxtaposed, the result is a four-quadrant framework. All people share characteristics of all four quadrants. However, individuals generally have a preferred quadrant that indicates what they most need when they enter a new learning experience. The preferences are described as Type One (Imaginative), Type Two (Analytic), Type Three (Common Sense), and Type Four (Dynamic).[17] (These types are explained further in the "Notes" section at the end of this chapter.) According to McCarthy, teachers do *not* need to test their students for learning-style preferences. The 4-MAT® model gives teachers a way to address learners' preferences by using the natural cycle that emerges from this framework. Learning for all learners begins in Quadrant One, with a connection to personal meaning. This personal connection leads the learner to Quadrant Two, with a need for conceptual understanding. This new understanding of expert knowledge leads the learner to Quadrant Three, with a need to try out these new concepts. In testing and trying new concepts, learners must move to Quadrant Four, with opportunities to adapt and integrate what they have learned.

The developers of the 4-MAT® System propose that when students are given the opportunity to learn in a natural cycle with the addition of a purposeful balance of right- and left-node instructional strategies in each of the four quadrants, their learning experiences will be complete and their personal engagement as learners will be ensured.

Similar Brains

Although all students learn and think differently, all brains are basically the same. Brain-based learning seeks to take what we know about the brain and apply it to education. Research shows that, among other things, the brain is social, it seeks meaning in everything, emotions affect its learning and thinking, challenge is good for the brain, and threat is bad.[18] One educator urges teachers to use this knowledge to create "intelligence-friendly classrooms" that foster "intelligent behavior for problem-solving, decision making, creative thinking . . . and the ongoing development of human potential."[19] Teachers build intelligence-friendly classrooms by: 1) Setting a safe emotional climate; 2) Creating a rich learning environment; 3) Teaching the mind-tools and skills of life; 4) Developing the skillfulness of the learner; 5) Challenging through the experience of doing; 6) Targeting multiple dimensions of intelligence; 7) Transferring learning through reflection; and 8) Balancing assessment measures.[20] By using these measures, which are based on what is known about the brain and how it works, teachers help all students be all they can be and reach their potential as learners and thinkers.

FOCUSING ON
THINKING SKILLS

When creating all the parts of effective learning experiences, teachers and library media specialists consider the instructional needs and goals, gather resources, plan teaching strategies, outline projects and activities, and, finally, examine the thinking skills being taught and learned. Thinking skills are crucial to information literacy development. Without thinking skills, students may learn facts, but will not know how to use them. Creative-thinking skills were discussed in chapter 6 along with problem solving. Critical-thinking skills are the focus of this section.

Bloom's Taxonomy

All learning and thinking are good, but some thinking is more challenging than other thinking. Benjamin Bloom categorized thinking into six levels: knowledge, comprehension, application, analysis, synthesis, and evaluation. Historically, Bloom's Taxonomy has been considered a hierarchy, with the levels increasing in difficulty. Today, some educators question this assumption. Many think two levels, synthesis and evaluation, are equal but require different thinking processes.[21] Others have found that students have less difficulty with these levels than with the lower levels of knowledge and comprehension.[22] Regardless of the order or levels of difficulty, Bloom's Taxonomy of thinking skills is beneficial to teachers and library media specialists because thinking skills are vital for information literacy development.

While acknowledging the importance of knowledge and comprehension in students' education, information literacy instruction emphasizes the higher levels of application, analysis, synthesis, and evaluation. These are the skills referred to by the information literacy indicator, "Uses information in critical thinking and problem solving" (standard 3, indicator 3). These also are the skills students will need to distinguish between fact and propaganda, develop presentations, design new systems or products, defend budgets or ideas, and be successful in their academic, professional, and personal lives.

Teaching Bloom

Each level of Bloom's Taxonomy is defined by certain tasks and thinking processes involved in completing those tasks. At the Knowledge stage, students are able to repeat information and label, name, list, or define it. At the Comprehension stage, students are able to understand information and can explain, paraphrase, or illustrate it. In the Application stage, students use information to complete a task and can demonstrate, compute, solve, and apply it. In the Analysis stage, students classify, compare, or organize information. Synthesis requires students to create, design, invent, or develop new ideas or products from information previously learned. Finally, the Evaluation stage requires students to critique or judge something using specific standards or criteria.[23]

Each level also is characterized by questions teachers ask to stimulate proper thinking processes and elicit appropriate responses from students.[24] Teaching, however, is more than just asking the right questions. It is giving students the tools to think with (graphic organizers) and showing them how to compare, contrast, and organize information. It is introducing the skills not in isolated lessons but in conjunction with other curriculum objectives. It is discussing, detailing, and modeling the critical-thinking skills. And it is giving students ample opportunities to practice thinking and constructing ideas in an unthreatening environment.

SUMMARY

Much thought goes into creating all the parts of a learning experience that will enhance students' information literacy development. Several issues deserve special consideration. These are the learning design process, the differences in learners, and the critical-thinking skills that are necessary for information literacy. Teachers and library media specialists collaborate in using problem-solving techniques to design lessons or thematic units. Considering the differences in learners (multiple intelligences and learning styles), the professionals build into the plan a variety of information sources, instructional presentation methods, activities, and evaluation projects. Finally, to foster information literacy, teachers and library media specialists provide opportunities for students to learn about, discuss, and use all levels of the critical-thinking skills represented by Bloom's Taxonomy of the Cognitive Domain.

NOTES

1. Daniel D. Barron, 1998, *Learning Design*. URL: http://www.libsci.sc.edu/dan/classes/jungle/learnd/index.htm. (Accessed November 8, 1999). Developed as an instructional tool for use with graduate students, the Learning Design Model is a graphical overview of the steps involved in creating effective learning experiences, the issues or considerations, and how they relate to each other and to the design process.

2. Ruth V. Small, 1998, *Designing Motivation into Library and Information Skills Instruction*. URL: http://www.ala.org/aasl/SLMQ/small.html. Reprinted by permission of the American Library Association. (Accessed November 8, 1999). In her online article, Small includes Abraham Maslow's Hierarchy of Needs in a discussion of the theories and concepts of motivation. She also discusses several instructional motivation models, giving details and examples of the ARCS Model of Motivational Design, and talks about the integration and application of motivation models in library and information skills instruction.

3.   From *Teaching with the Brain in Mind* by Eric Jensen. Alexandria, VA: Association for Supervision and Curriculum Development. Copyright © 1998 ASCD. Reprinted by permission. All rights reserved. Jensen includes a chapter titled "How Threats and Stress Affect Learning." In his advice to educators, Jensen suggests ways to "manage the conditions that can induce" stress and ways to "use personal strategies that mediate and release it" (from "Practical Suggestions," page 59).

4.   Howard E. Gardner, *Frames of Mind: The Theory of Multiple Intelligences*, Tenth Anniversary Edition (New York: Basic Books, 1993). Used by permission. Gardner explains his theory of multiple intelligences and gives examples of seven intelligences identified at this point.

5.   Susan Brooks, 1996, *Ornaments—Gardner's Seven Intelligences*. URL: http://monster. educ.kent.edu/deafed/96-08-d.htm. (Accessed November 8, 1999). This site gives a concise definition of each of the first seven intelligences.

6.   Zephyr Press, 1998–99, *Multiple Intelligences: An Interview with Howard Gardner*. URL: http://www.zephyrpress.com/gardner.htm. (Accessed November 8, 1999). Reprinted by permission. Ronnie Durie, editor of *Mindshift Connection*, talks with Howard Gardner about the eighth intelligence—the naturalist—and the implications of the MI movement on education.

7.   Ibid.

8.   Shirley A. Griggs, "Learning Styles Counseling," *ERIC Clearinghouse on Counseling and Personnel Services* (December 31, 1991): n.p. This article is included in Selected ERIC Abstracts on Learning Styles (http://www.ascd.org/services/eric/ericlngs.html) and gives an overview of several different learning style models and the characteristics stressed by each.

9.   Dawna Markova, 1996, *A Symphony of Learning Styles*. URL: http://www.weac. org/kids/june96/styles.htm. (Accessed November 8, 1999). Reprinted by permission of *On WEAC*. Sponsored by the Wisconsin Education Association Council, this site explains learning styles as the combination of a person's perceptual pathway to learning (visual, kinesthetic, auditory) and the particular state of consciousness (conscious, subconscious, unconscious) of each. The six patterns are explained and illustrated in an effort to help teachers "help children think and learn to the best of their abilities," and to "understand behaviors that might stand in the way of learning."

10.   Ibid.

11.   Daniel D. Barron, "Doing It with Style or Different Strokes for Different Folks: Learning Styles for School Library Media Specialists," *School Library Media Activities Monthly* 14 (October 1997): 48–50. Used with permission. In his column, "Keeping Current," Dr. Barron discusses personality types, learner differences, and learning style inventories, giving references for further reading. He mentions the 4-MAT® System and includes this quote from its developer, Bernice McCarthy: "Teachers need not label learners according to their style, just help them work for balance and wholeness."

12.   Cynthia Wilson, n.d., *Learning Styles*. URL: http://www.geocities.com/CollegePark/ Union/2106/ls.html. (Accessed November 8, 1999). Used with permission. Part of "The Education Place," a Web site developed for and maintained by North Carolina educators, this segment focuses on learning styles and the model and inventory developed by Dr. Rita Dunn. Background information is found through "The Basics" link, and a wealth of other resources are accessible through the link, "Learning Styles Connections."

13.   Wichita Public Schools, USD 259, "Learning Skills Inventory," in *Running a School Library Media Center: A How-To-Do-It Manual for Librarians*, by Barbara L. Stein and Risa W. Brown (New York: Neal-Schuman, 1992). This inventory includes the survey, an answer sheet, and a worksheet for determining students' styles.

14.   Ibid., 89.

15.   Richard E. Snow, "Aptitudes and Symbol Systems in Adaptive Classroom Teaching," *Phi Delta Kappan* 78 (January 1997): 354–60. Copyright © *Phi Delta Kappan*. Reprinted by permission. The exact quote (found on page 359) states that "there appears to be some benefit in matching symbol systems and ability profiles, at least for immediate learning. That is, for immediate results, it may be better to give more verbal elaboration to more verbal students and more figural elaboration to more spatial students. But the opposite may be best if longer-term retention is the goal. It is possible that mismatching symbol-system and aptitude profile can provide a kind of compensatory elaboration."

16.   About Learning, Inc., 1999, *About Learning, Inc.: To Make Learning Meaningful and Equitable*. URL: http://www.aboutlearning.com. (Accessed November 8, 1999). This is the official site of the 4-MAT® System for Teaching and Learning. Links in the document include "What Is 4-MAT®?" and "4-MAT® and Multiple Intelligences." A quote from one page highlights the relationship of the model to information literacy: "Our goal is to do more than just fill students with facts. Our goal is to train them to think and learn well and to exercise competent judgment in multiple situations."

17.   Ibid. Four different types of learning preferences are recognized by the 4-MAT® System. Type One (Imaginative) Learners perceive through sensing/feeling and process by reflecting. They are primarily interested in personal meaning. To reach these students, teachers must create a reason for learning. Type Two (Analytic) Learners perceive through thinking and process by reflecting. They are primarily interested in expert knowledge to increase their understanding. To reach these learners, teachers must provide them with the facts. Type Three (Common Sense) Learners perceive by thinking and process by doing. They are primarily interested in how things work. They need hands-on activities. Type Four (Dynamic) Learners perceive by sensing/feeling and process by acting. They are primarily interested in self-discovery. They want to take risks, try new things for themselves, and then share their new learning with others.

18.   From *Education on the Edge of Possibility* by Renate Nummela Caine and Geoffrey Caine. Alexandria, VA: Association for Supervision and Curriculum Development. Copyright © 1997 ASCD. Used by permission. All rights reserved. In Section 1—Theory: The Foundation—Caine and Caine present twelve Brain/Mind Learning Principles, which are the basis of brain-based instruction. Other sections in this book include Practice

and Implementation and What We Learned. The content is based on the authors' experiences implementing brain-based learning in two schools.

19.   Robin Fogarty, "The Intelligence-Friendly Classroom: It Just Makes Sense," *Phi Delta Kappan* 79 (May 1998): 655–57. Copyright © 1998 by Skylight Training and Publishing, Inc. Reprinted by permission. In her article, Ms. Fogarty defines an intelligence-friendly classroom, gives the theoretical underpinnings for the guidelines, suggests implications for application, and concludes by saying the intelligence-friendly classroom "draws on the many powers of intelligence of both the teacher and the learner. . . . It is the science of good, sound pedagogy coupled with the art of uniquely creative minds. . . . It's about children, and it's about helping those children be as smart as they can be in every way they can be. The intelligence-friendly classroom just makes sense" (page 657).

20.   Ibid., 656–57.

21.   William Huitt, 1998, *Bloom et al.'s Taxonomy of the Cognitive Domain.* URL: http://chiron.valdosta.edu/whuitt/col/cogsys/bloom.html. (Accessed November 8, 1999). Used by permission. Bill Huitt's Web site gives background information on the original document by Bloom and others, and includes a chart depicting each level of Bloom's Taxonomy, a definition of that level in terms of student abilities (student recalls, student translates, etc.), sample verbs that can be used to elicit the proper level of response, and sample behaviors or student objectives.

22.   Phyllis P. Bray and Jeanne M. Rogers, *Ideas in Bloom: Taxonomy-Based Activities for U.S. Studies* (Portland, ME: J. Weston Walch, 1995), 3. Courtesy of J. Weston Walch, Publisher © 1995. This book also gives an analysis of the six levels in Bloom's Taxonomy. In addition, it offers ideas for activities in all six realms of thinking. All the activities are based on U.S. social studies topics and are supported with teachers' notes and answers for the activity pages. Not only are the suggestions excellent but they offer models for teachers and library media specialists to use when designing thinking activities for other subjects.

23.   William Huitt, 1998, *Bloom et al.'s Taxonomy of the Cognitive Domain.* URL: http://chiron.valdosta.edu/whuitt/col/cogsys/bloom.html. (Accessed November 8, 1999). See Note 21.

24.   John Maynard, n.d., *Bloom's Taxonomy's Model Questions and Key Words.* URL: http://www.utexas.edu/student/lsc/handouts/1414.html. (Accessed August 28, 1999). Provided by the University of Texas at Austin's Learning Skills Center. This document is very helpful for teachers and library media specialists who want to develop critical-thinking activities in conjunction with thematic units. Examples of the keywords or questions are 1) Knowledge—who, what, choose, define, what does it mean?; 2) Comprehension—explain, give an example, what would happen if?; 3) Application—predict what would happen if, tell how much change there would be; 4) Analysis—distinguish, what does author believe?, the least essential statements are; 5) Synthesis—create, design, how else would you?; 6) Evaluation—judge, defend, which is more important?

ADDITIONAL READINGS

Bunch, John. 1998. *Creative and Critical Thinking*. URL: http://curry.edschool.virginia. edu/curry/class/Museums/Teacher_Guide/Time_Line/creativethinking.html. Accessed November 8, 1999. This Web address is for the Field Trip Planning Guide Time Line of the *Going to a Museum? A Teacher's Guide* Web site. Follow the link to "Creative and Critical Thinking." This page suggests critical-thinking activities for students who are visiting a museum. The ideas presented here can be used in other situations as well.

Carr, Kathryn S. "How Can We Teach Critical Thinking?" *Childhood Education* (Winter 1988): 69–73. This article is reproduced as an ERIC Digest (ED 326 304) and is found on the Internet at http://www.valdosta.peachnet.edu/~whuitt/psy702/digests/ critthnk.dig. Carr presents the need for teaching critical-thinking skills and offers ways to integrate them into reading, writing, and classification activities. The author concludes with the following statement: "The urgent need to teach thinking skills at all levels of education continues. But we should not rely on special courses and texts to do the job. Instead, every teacher should create an atmosphere where students are encouraged to read deeply, question, engage in divergent thinking, look for relationships among ideas, and grapple with real life issues."

Carvin, Andy. N.d. *MI—The Theory*. URL: http://edweb.gsn.org/edref.mi.th.html. Accessed November 8, 1999. This site provides links to descriptions of seven of Gardner's intelligences, and other articles about MI theory.

Cerny, Jerry. N.d. *Question Types Based on Bloom's Taxonomy*. URL: http://www.hcc. hawaii.edu/intranet/committees/FacDevCom/guidebk/teachtip/questype.htm. Accessed November 8, 1999. Directed to teachers, this site lists the six levels of thinking, the skills needed for each, and the types of questions to ask in each category.

Huitt, William G. 1998. *Maslow's Hierarchy of Needs*. URL: http://www.valdosta.peachnet. edu/~whuitt/psy702/regsys/maslow.html. Accessed November 8, 1999. This site contains explanations of Maslow's Hierarchy of Needs and Alderfer's Hierarchy of Motivational Needs and discusses some other motivational theories.

Chapter 8

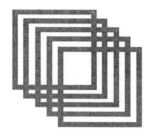

Making It All Work

*Learning is not attained by chance,
it must be sought for with ardor and
attended to with diligence.*

—Abigail Adams

CHECKLIST OF INFORMATION GOALS, OBJECTIVES, AND STRATEGIES

Information literacy instruction cannot be left to chance, either. For it to be effective, teachers and library media specialists must develop a school-wide systematic plan to ensure that all the necessary skills and objectives are being taught and practiced. This chapter provides the Checklist of Information Literacy Goals, Objectives, and Strategies to aid in planning and in record keeping. Teachers and library media specialists can consult the checklist for ideas about activities related to specific information literacy objectives and, by checking off skills as they are introduced, keep track of what has been taught and discussed and what has not.

The Checklist of Information Literacy Goals, Objectives, and Strategies is divided into four sections. These segments correspond to the AASL/AECT Information Literacy Standards for Student Learning. The first section focuses on skills and activities connected with the research process. The second offers ideas for fostering independent learning. The third section concentrates on fostering attitudes related to responsible and ethical behavior in the use of information and information technology. The last one provides activities to promote appropriate group participation.

The checklist is an adaptation of the AASL/AECT Information Literacy Standards for Student Learning. Each standard is considered an instructional goal. Each indicator is considered an objective, and the activities listed beneath are the strategies for achieving those goals and objectives. The blank spaces in each section are for teachers and library media specialists to add their own ideas and activities. The Checklist of Information Literacy Goals, Objectives, and Strategies is included in the disk that came with this book.

(Text continues on page 125.)

Table 8.1
Checklist of Information Literacy Goals, Objectives, and Strategies

A. FOSTERING THE RESEARCH PROCESS	Unit/Date	Unit/Date	Unit/Date
GOAL/Objective/Strategies			
1. ACCESS INFORMATION EFFICIENTLY/EFFECTIVELY			
1.1. Recognizes need for information			
Pre-test			
Problem solving			
Assignments involve personal interests			
Class/small-group discussion			
Guiding questions			
Cooperative groups			
Brainstorming sessions			
1.2. Recognizes accurate and comprehensive information is basis for intelligent decision making			
Discuss article reviews			
Discuss book reviews			
Evaluate print resources			
Evaluate nonprint resources			
Evaluate Internet resources			
Authority			
Copyright date			
Compare/contrast resources			
1.3. Formulates questions based on information needs			
Guiding questions			
Narrow topic			
Broaden topic			
Keyword development			
Evaluation rubric for process			

From *Fostering Information Literacy: Connecting National Standards, Goals 2000, and the SCANS Report.* © 2000 Libraries Unlimited. (800) 237-6124.

A. FOSTERING THE RESEARCH PROCESS	Unit/Date	Unit/Date	Unit/Date
GOAL/Objective/Strategies			
1.4. Identifies variety of potential sources of information			
Print			
Reference sources			
Journal articles			
Newspapers			
Telephone book			
Nonfiction books			
Nonprint			
Cable programs			
ETV/ITV programs			
Videotapes			
Audiotapes			
Photographs			
Interviews			
Field trips			
Computer-related			
InfoTrac			
Electric library			
CD-ROMs			
Internet			
1.5. Develops/uses successful strategies for locating information			
Search strategies			
Keyword search development			
Call number knowledge			
Table of contents			
Indexes			
Bibliographies			

A. FOSTERING THE RESEARCH PROCESS	Unit/Date	Unit/Date	Unit/Date
GOAL/Objective/Strategies			
Online catalog			
Computer navigation knowledge			
Internet			
Search engines			
Boolean operators			
Links			
2. EVALUATES INFORMATION CRITICALLY AND COMPETENTLY			
2.1. Determines accuracy, relevance, and comprehensiveness			
Book reviews			
Comparison/contrast of sources			
Evaluation rubric for relevance			
2.2. Distinguishes among fact, point of view, and opinion			
Comparison/contrast of sources			
Authority publishers			
Primary/secondary sources			
2.3. Identifies inaccurate and misleading information			
Authority publishers			
Compare/contrast sources			
Internet			
Copyright dates			
2.4. Selects information appropriate to the problem or question at hand			
Guiding questions			
Evaluation rubric for process			
Rough drafts/editing			

A. *FOSTERING THE RESEARCH PROCESS*	Unit/Date	Unit/Date	Unit/Date
GOAL/Objective/Strategies			
Additional information			
Graphic organizers			
3. USES INFORMATION EFFECTIVELY AND CREATIVELY			
3.1. Organizes information for practical application			
Graphic organizers			
Note cards/Web pages			
Evaluation rubric for product			
Time lines			
3.2. Integrates new information into one's own knowledge			
Generates original reports			
Portfolios			
Fictional diaries			
Plays			
Stories			
News reports			
Post-tests			
3.3. Applies information in critical thinking and problem solving			
Uses knowledge across subject areas			
Real-world assignments			
Problem-solving curriculum			
Relevant research			
Data collection			
Observations			
Conclusions			

A. *FOSTERING THE RESEARCH PROCESS*	Unit/Date	Unit/Date	Unit/Date
GOAL/Objective/Strategies			
Analyze data			
Spreadsheets			
Databases			
3.4. Produces and communicates information and ideas in appropriate formats			
Portfolios			
Videos			
Presentations with computer software			
Written reports			
Multimedia presentations			
Posters			
Collages			
Overheads			
Skits			
Musical presentations			
Visual art displays (paintings, sculpture, etc.)			
Speeches			

B. FOSTERING INDEPENDENT LEARNING	Unit/Date	Unit/Date	Unit/Date
GOAL/Objective/Strategies			
4. PURSUES INFORMATION RELATED TO PERSONAL INTERESTS			
4.1. Seeks information related to various dimensions of personal well-being, such as career interests, community involvement, health matters, and recreational pursuits			
Accesses other libraries			
Silent sustained reading			
Drop Everything and Read (DEAR)			
Accelerated reader program			
Book clubs			
Community service			
Mentor/intern program			
Career research			
Career shadowing			
School-to-work activities			
Collaboration with business partners			
4.2. Designs, develops, and evaluates information products and solutions related to personal interests			
Independent projects			
Develops Web page			
Publishes newspaper			
Writes articles, editorials			
Evaluates media information (media literacy)			
5. APPRECIATES AND ENJOYS LITERATURE AND OTHER CREATIVE EXPRESSIONS OF INFORMATION			
5.1. Competent and self-motivated reader			
Flexible scheduling			
Sustained silent reading			

B. FOSTERING INDEPENDENT LEARNING	Unit/Date	Unit/Date	Unit/Date
GOAL/Objective/Strategies			
Drop Everything and Read (DEAR)			
Accelerated reader program			
Book talks			
Book clubs			
Guest Reader Day			
Use of novels to introduce/enhance units			
5.2. Derives meaning from information presented in a variety of formats			
Books			
Magazine articles			
Newspapers			
Telephone directory			
Diaries			
Maps			
Other original documents			
Videos			
ETV/ITV programs			
Filmstrips			
Photographs/slides			
Hyperstudio/PowerPoint presentation			
CD-ROM			
Internet			
Play/skit			
5.3. Develops creative products in a variety of formats			
Publish book			
Write magazine article			
Publish newspaper			
Keep hypothetical diary			
Write poetry			

From *Fostering Information Literacy: Connecting National Standards, Goals 2000, and the SCANS Report.* © 2000 Libraries Unlimited. (800) 237-6124.

B. *FOSTERING INDEPENDENT LEARNING*	Unit/Date	Unit/Date	Unit/Date
GOAL/Objective/Strategies			
Produce video			
Develop Hyperstudio stack			
Develop PowerPoint presentation			
Produce audiotape			
Produce play/skit/newscast			
Use photographs			
Develop Web page			
6. STRIVES FOR EXCELLENCE IN INFORMATION SEEKING AND KNOWLEDGE GENERATION			
6.1. Assesses quality of process and product of own information seeking			
Evaluation rubric for process			
Evaluation rubric for product			
Seeks feedback			
Revisions			
6.2. Devises strategies for revising, improving, and updating self-generated knowledge			
Rough drafts/editing			
Add information			
Databases			
Spreadsheets			
Broaden/narrow topic			
Controversial subjects/changing opinions			
Outdated versus current information			
Current events			
Research journals			
Follow-up activities			

C. FOSTERING RESPONSIBLE AND ETHICAL BEHAVIOR	Unit/Date	Unit/Date	Unit/Date
GOAL/Objective/Strategies			
7. RECOGNIZES IMPORTANCE OF INFORMATION TO A DEMOCRATIC SOCIETY			
7.1. Seeks information from diverse sources, contexts, disciplines, and cultures			
Print			
Nonprint			
Language arts			
Social studies			
Science			
Math			
Fine arts			
Health			
Home arts			
Physical education			
Clubs			
Newscasts/newscasters			
Multicultural emphasis			
Hispanic-American Month			
Black History Month			
7.2. Respects principle of equitable access to information			
All resources available to all students			
Flexible scheduling			
Guided discussions			
Handicap access			

From *Fostering Information Literacy: Connecting National Standards, Goals 2000, and the SCANS Report.* © 2000 Libraries Unlimited. (800) 237-6124.

C. FOSTERING RESPONSIBLE AND ETHICAL BEHAVIOR	Unit/Date	Unit/Date	Unit/Date
GOAL/Objective/Strategies			
8. PRACTICES ETHICAL BEHAVIOR IN REGARD TO INFORMATION AND INFORMATION TECHNOLOGY			
8.1. Respects principles of intellectual freedom			
Students select own books and resources			
Guided discussions			
Banned-book discussions			
Community concerns discussions			
Book/media selection policies			
8.2. Respects intellectual property rights			
Copyright laws			
Plagiarism			
Paraphrase			
Quotations			
Bibliographies			
8.3. Uses information technology responsibly			
Internet Use Agreement			
E-mail etiquette			
Copyright laws			
Bibliographies			
Proper computer use and care			

D. FOSTERING GROUP PARTICIPATION	Unit/Date	Unit/Date	Unit/Date
GOAL/Objective/Strategies			
9. PARTICIPATES EFFECTIVELY IN GROUPS TO PURSUE AND GENERATE INFORMATION			
9.1. Shares knowledge and information with others			
Cooperative groups			
E-mail			
Web pages			
Jigsaw units			
Cooperative comprehensive searches			
E-mail pals			
Interschool collaborative projects			
9.2. Respects others' ideas and backgrounds and acknowledges their contributions			
Cooperative groups			
Class/small-group discussions			
Multicultural emphasis			
Yearlong integration			
Multicultural resources			
Multicultural guest speakers			
9.3. Collaborates with others, both in person and through technologies, to identify information problems and to seek their solutions			
Problem-solving curriculum and activities			
Cooperative groups			
E-mail projects			
Internet projects			
Interschool			
International			
With organizations			

From *Fostering Information Literacy: Connecting National Standards, Goals 2000, and the SCANS Report.* © 2000 Libraries Unlimited. (800) 237-6124.

D. FOSTERING GROUP PARTICIPATION	Unit/Date	Unit/Date	Unit/Date
GOAL/Objective/Strategies			
9.4. Collaborates with others, both in person and through technologies, to design, develop, and evaluate information products and solutions			
Cooperative groups			
E-mail projects			
Internet projects			
Problem-solving curriculum and activities			
Creative products			
Evaluation rubrics			
Community involvement			

ADDITIONAL READINGS

K-W-L-H Charts

Presseisen, Barbara Z. 1995. *K-W-L-H Technique*. URL: http://www.ncrel.org/sdrs/areas/issues/students/learning/lr1kwlh.htm. Accessed August 28, 1999. This link from a NCREL Critical Issues site describes the K-W-L-H teaching technique developed by Donna Ogle in 1986. Students create a chart listing what they know (K), what they want to learn (W), what they learned (L), and how they can learn more (H).

Opinion Indicators

Larson, Randy J. *How to Write Reports: A Guide for Grades 6–9.* Portland, ME: J. Weston Walch, 1991, 12. The list of opinion indicators in the checklist comes from this book. Although it is written for grades 6–9, many of the ideas can be used with younger students. The book is designed to be used by students (reproducible worksheets), and its humorous approach to writing reports keeps students interested.

Question-Answer Relationships

Ouzts, Dan T. "Enhancing the Connection Between Literature and the Social Studies Using the Question-Answer Relationship." *Social Studies and the Young Learner* (March/April 1998): 26–28. This article describes the Question-Answer Relationship (QAR) instructional activity, which was developed by Taffy Raphael. The activity focuses on categorizing questions about a particular text (story or nonfiction). The teacher-generated questions are either text-based (referred to as "Right There" and "Think and Search") or knowledge-based ("Author & Me" and "On My Own"). Students must decide whether the answer to a question is found in the book or in their heads (prior knowledge).

Other

Presseisen, Barbara Z. 1995. *Critical Issue: Building on Prior Knowledge and Meaningful Student Contexts/Cultures*. URL: http://www.ncrel.org/sdrs/areas/issues/students/learning/lr100.htm. Accessed November 8, 1999. Part of the NCREL Internet site, this article discusses the issue of students' prior knowledge and its importance to student learning. The article includes an overview of the issue, opinions by educators, strategies, pitfalls, and opposing viewpoints.

Rowan, Kelly Jo. n.d. *Glossary of Instructional Strategies*. URL: http://www.cs.utk.edu/~rowan/edu/teaching.htm#S. Accessed November 8, 1999. This alphabetized list gives brief descriptions of many instructional strategies and occasionally includes a link to a related Web site.

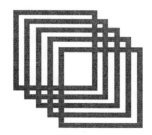

Chapter **9**

Some Examples

Example is always more efficacious than precept.
—Samuel Johnson

This chapter contains four unit plans that integrate information literacy skills and objectives with other subject-area objectives. The plans follow the outline presented in the Lesson Plan Model and represent elements included in the graphic Learning Design Model. The information literacy goals and objectives are taken from the AASL/AECT Information Literacy Standards for Student Learning, and the subject-area objectives are taken from the corresponding national curriculum standards. The units may be modified and adapted to meet the needs of students slightly above or below the targeted grade level.

SAMPLE INTEGRATED
LESSON PLAN I—INVENTIONS

Grade Level 5: Needs Assessment

The Language Arts National Standards state:

1. Students apply a wide range of strategies to comprehend, interpret, evaluate, and appreciate texts.

2. Students conduct research on issues and interests by generating ideas and questions and by posing problems.

3. Students use a variety of technological and informational resources to gather and synthesize data.

From past reports and tests, teachers have observed that their students lack knowledge of the steps necessary in accessing and evaluating information to produce a comprehensive, creative product.

The National Science Standards state:

1. Students should identify a simple problem and then identify a specific task and solution related to the problem.

2. Students should make proposals to build something or get something to work better.

3. Students should be able to evaluate a product or design by evaluating their own results or solutions to problems by considering how well a product or design met the challenge to solve a problem.

Background Information

These students will be studying inventions and inventors. This integrated unit will be taught by the science and language arts teachers. In science, the students will create their own inventions. In language arts, the students will research an invention that they choose and create a scrapbook about the invention and its inventor(s). Extra credit will be given for creating an advertisement jingle or postage stamp showing or marketing the invention.

Goals and Objectives

Language Arts Goals

1. Students will understand the steps necessary in researching a topic.

2. Students will demonstrate the ability to locate and access at least three different sources from print materials, CD-ROMs, InfoTrac, and the Internet.

3. Students will evaluate those materials and be able to extrapolate important facts from those sources.

Language Arts Objectives

1. Students will demonstrate the ability to use SIRS Discoverer and Info-Trak, and to select and use print materials independently.

2. Students will develop an overview note sheet with information they have selected from a variety of formats—print, nonprint, and electronic.

3. Students will condense the information from various sources and synthesize that information into a logical report.

Information Literacy Goals

1. Students will access reference materials effectively.

2. Students will evaluate information and choose material appropriately.

3. Students will use information creatively in producing their finished project.

Information Literacy Objectives

1. Students will be able to formulate questions based on their information needs.

2. Students will be able to select information that best answers their query.

3. Students will be able to synthesize information from a variety of resources.

4. Students will be able to create their project using the information gathered and present their final product to the class.

Science Goals

1. Students will understand the different types of inventions (machines, clothes, furniture, etc.).

2. Students will understand the link between simple and complex machines.

Science Objectives

1. Students will decide what type of invention they want to create.

2. Students will demonstrate knowledge of the steps in creating an invention by creating their own.

Information Literacy Goals

1. Students will strive for excellence in producing their invention.

2. Students will apply skills in problem solving.

Information Literacy Objectives

1. Students will be able to assess the quality of their invention and make needed improvements.

2. Students will be able to integrate information learned about past inventions in creating their own invention.

Preparation

The library media center is to be fully involved in this unit. The library media specialist (LMS) will meet with the teachers and discuss the objectives in science and math and what role the LMS and the teachers will play. A timeline and a beginning and culminating activity will be prepared.

Responsibilities

Classroom Teacher

1. The language arts (LA) teacher will be responsible for making sure the student has the right amount of sources.

2. The LA teacher will make sure the students understand the process of combining their information into a cohesive report.

3. The LA teacher will instruct the students in how he or she wants the scrapbook prepared.

4. The science teacher will be responsible for helping the students in understanding how to problem solve.

5. The science teacher will conduct small-group brainstorming sessions to help students in understanding the steps in creating an invention.

Library Media Specialist

1. Students will come to the library media center in groups of six. The LMS will evaluate what information they already possess about their inventions and what they need to find out. The students will write down keywords concerning their invention to start their search.

2. The LMS will introduce the Overview Note Sheet[1] and instruct students in how to use it.

3. The LMS will instruct the students on the use of SIRS Discoverer and InfoTrak.

4. The LMS will instruct the students on the use of various print materials and how to use indexes and cross-references.

5. The LMS will assist students in learning how to take notes from the print materials, using the outline from *Brainstorms and Blueprints*; she will show students how to print out information from InfoTrac, SIRS Discoverer, and Grolier Multimedia Encyclopedia.

6. The LMS will contact members of the community and coordinate the Invention Convention.

Resources and Materials

Print resources—reference, fiction, biography, nonfiction, poetry.

Nonprint resources—CD-ROM on Leonardo da Vinci, SIRS Discoverer, Grolier Multimedia Encyclopedia, InfoTrac

Set of videos on inventions

Posters showing six simple machines

Overheads

Banners

Boxes, garbage bags and ties, duct tape (for invention in library media center)

Letters to community volunteers and parents

Activities

Science

1. Students will come to the media center for a lesson on the steps in creating an invention and discussion about different types of inventions.

2. Students and the LMS will create their own invention.

3. Students will use resources the LMS has collected for them to help them create their own invention.

Language Arts

1. Students will come to the media center in small groups to look at various resources and gather information.

2. Students will collect information and take notes from their information sources.

3. Students will create note cards with bibliographic information on each resource.

4. Students will produce a scrapbook about their inventor.

Evaluation

Language Arts

Excellent

- Student has a well-written, logical, and cohesive report.

- Student has used more than three citations or sources.

- Student has used print and nonprint sources for the report.

- The scrapbook is neat, organized, and creative.

Adequate

- Student has written a report that cites two sources.

- Student used a print and nonprint source for information.

- Student's report is organized, but doesn't contain all the information necessary about the invention and the inventor.

- Student's scrapbook is organized, but lacks creativity.

Inadequate

- Student has used fewer than two sources.

- Student used print resource only to gather information.

- Student's report contains only the "bare bones" about the invention/inventor.

- Student's scrapbook lacks creativity and is not organized.

Science

Excellent

- Student's invention is original, creative, and solves a need.

- Student used "everyday" materials (e.g., paper, foils, boxes, bags, wires, pins, etc.) in a unique way.

Adequate

- Student's invention is a re-creation of an existing invention, but is done in a creative way.

- Student used some original material and some bought (e.g., models).

Inadequate:

- Student's invention lacks originality and creativity.

- Student used purchased materials (e.g., models, posters, prepackaged materials).

Follow-up Activity

An "Invention Convention" will be held at the end of the unit. Members of the community and parents will be invited to participate. The students' inventions will be displayed. Community members will display inventions or improvements to inventions in their particular fields. Businesses such as the telephone company, extension agencies, the fire department, the police dive team, a medical library, a television channel's weather department, and the local newspaper will be invited to display. The newspaper will print an article about the event.

SAMPLE INTEGRATED
LESSON PLAN II—CHINA

Grade Level 4: Needs Assessment

The National History Standard 7 states that students should understand selected attributes and historical developments of societies in such places as Africa, the Americas, Asia, and Europe. The English Language Arts Standard 7 states that students should conduct research on issues and interests by generating ideas and questions, and by posing problems. They gather, evaluate, and synthesize data from a variety of sources to communicate their discoveries in ways that suit their purpose and audience.

The Arts Music Standard 7 states that students should understand the relationship between music and history and culture.

The Arts Visual Arts Standard 4 states that students should understand the visual arts in relation to history and cultures.

The Arts Dance Standard 5 states that students understand dance in various cultures and historical periods.

From classroom discussions, the fourth-grade teachers recognize that their students know very little about China. In art and music classes, China has never been discussed before; the teachers will start with videos about China so that the students will gain some background knowledge about the country before exploring the arts.

Background Information

The fourth-graders at Jeff's school are involved in a study of China. The following scenarios show how China is being studied in class, in the media center, in art, in music, and in P.E. (physical education). In addition, Jeff's research on China shows how he needs information literacy skills, language arts skills, history skills, and fine arts skills to complete his work.

Goals and Objectives

History Goals

In history, students will understand the culture and history of China.

History Objectives

1. Students will be able to describe the Chinese way of life.

2. Students will be able to describe how the geography of China creates the very different ways that people live in the various regions of that country.

3. Students will be able to analyze the arts of China and draw conclusions about how the arts tie in with the culture.

Language Arts Goals

Students will use research skills to gather information for a report on their topics of study concerning China.

Language Arts Objectives

1. Students will appreciate the literature—folklore, poetry—of China.

2. Students will use fiction, nonfiction, and reference sources in gathering information on China.

3. Students will demonstrate how to use CD-ROMs, the Internet, interviews, and print text in producing their reports.

Fine Arts Goals

Students will make a connection between the culture of China and the art and music of its people.

Fine Arts Objectives

1. Students will know the cultural context of the Lion Dance and the historical background of this dance.

2. Students will understand the different rhythmic and melodic sounds that create the unique Chinese music.

3. Students will know and be able to identify Chinese brush art.

Information Literacy Goals

1. Students will locate and synthesize information gathered on China.

2. Students will use the information gathered in creating a finished product.

3. Students will appreciate the literature, music, dance, and art of China.

4. Students will work together in collecting information and creating material to share with others.

Information Literacy Objectives

1. Students will be able to identify a variety of resources and develop search strategies for gathering information from those resources.

2. Students will be able to organize the information collected and produce a creative and appropriate product for sharing with others.

3. Students will be able to understand and appreciate the meaning of Chinese literature, art, and music through their study of the Chinese arts.

4. Students will be able to work collaboratively in producing a musical production featuring artwork and the Lion Dance.

Responsibilites

Classroom Teacher

1. Introduce the topic and geography information.

2. Arrange for guest speaker.

3. Assist students in creating final report.

Library Media Specialist

1. Assist students in small groups to gather information about China.

2. Teach students how to narrow the search, select a topic, and gather information from various resources.

3. Assist students in taking notes from their resources.

4. Show students how to use CD-ROMs and the Internet.

5. Help students evaluate correct and incorrect information.

Art Teacher

1. The art teacher reviews the history and background of brush painting and discusses the techniques.

2. The teacher instructs the students in how to create a brush painting.

3. The teacher shows the students how to create a 3-D dragon.

Music Teacher

1. The music teacher introduces the music, instruments, and rhythms in Chinese music.

2. The teacher instructs students in the history of the Lion Dance and its symbolism in Chinese culture.

3. The teacher introduces the instruments and instructs the students in creating a composition to accompany the Lion Dance.

4. The teacher shows the students the dance and instructs them in the movements.

P.E. Teacher

1. The P.E. teacher introduces two games played in China.

2. The teacher shows the students how to play the games.

Resources and Materials

Classroom

Maps

Globe

Geography handout

Internet pictures of the Great Wall

CD-ROMs

Items from home that were made in China

Chinese food

Library Media Center

Encyclopedias, atlases, almanacs, works of fiction and nonfiction

Paper and pencil

CD-ROMs, Internet access

Art

Movies

Picture of a Chinese dragon

Book: *Dragons, Unicorns & Other Magical Beasts*

Construction paper

Paint

Bulletin-board paper

Basket reeds

String

Crepe streamers

Scissors, glue, paintbrushes

Music

Orff instruments

Song: "Mongolian Night Song"

P.E.

Jump rope

Ribbons

Activities

Classroom

In the classroom, the teacher introduces the study of China by discussing China's location. The students look at a map of the world and see where this country is. They talk about the size of China, and the teacher introduces some facts about the land area, population, and government of China. The teacher then introduces map terms such as *latitude, longitude, prime meridian, equator*. The teacher defines the words and conducts a class discussion about them. Ms. Lufton has prepared a handout for the students to study. This handout has the country of China with the map markings on it, as well as a key. She plays a game with the students by having them locate different cities and landmarks on the map using latitude and longitude. This map also contains topographical information, and the class discusses the features of China—mountains, lakes, rivers. They have fun with the pronunciation of some of the names! Ms. Lufton has also downloaded some pictures from the Internet of the Great Wall of China, which she shares with the class. The students are fascinated with this landmark and the teacher tells the class about the wall, how it was built, how long it took, etc. Because of the interest of some of the students, after the discussion the teacher allows them to look up more information about the Great Wall on the Internet and on an encyclopedia CD-ROM.

The next day, the class shares a Chinese take-out meal from a nearby restaurant that the teacher has brought in. Ms. Lufton has talked with the restaurant owners and one of them has agreed to come and talk with the class about China and then to answer questions. In preparation for this, each student will have to write down one question he or she would like to have answered about China. Ms. Lufton will check those questions before Mr. Ling's visit. After his visit, the students will have to write down what they learned and identify other questions they would like answered. This will help them to prepare for the research project.

Mr. Ling is a wonderful visitor. He brings with him a Chinese silk jacket and chopsticks for everyone! The students have great fun trying to follow Mr. Ling's directions about how to use the chopsticks. The students ask Mr. Ling about the different types of foods they've heard about—such as Mongolian and Hunan. Mr. Ling talks about the different geographical locations and how the area you live in affects your food, music, clothes, etc. He relates this idea to the students by talking about how certain foods—like grits—are associated with the South in the United States. They take a vote and decide to eat lunch in the cafeteria with the chopsticks. Ms. Lufton has also brought some items that were made in China to share with the class.

When her students have gathered all their information on China—from class and from work in the library media center—Ms. Lufton then leads them through the process of creating a finished product. In small groups, she works with them in creating an opening paragraph, the body of their report, and their conclusions. When the reports are finished, the students will present their reports orally to their classmates. The class will take information from each report and generate a "class list" of ideas and information they have learned about China. This list will be displayed outside the class in the hallway.

Library Media Center

In the library media center, the students are working with the library media specialist on a research project on China. They go to the library media center in small groups to work on this project. On their first visit, they talk about narrowing the focus of their study, for China itself is far too big a subject area. The LMS leads them through different exercises, such as creating a web and writing down all the words they can think of that are associated with China. After that, they talk about the different areas of interest chosen from the web of keywords they have generated. They pick different areas to study, such as government, way of life, or land and arts. Each student decides which topic he or she would like to study. They then look through the different resources available in their library and take notes on which sources have information on their subject. They look through the encyclopedias and note the volume and page numbers where they can find information. The students then look through the almanacs and atlases. Some find useful information on their topics; some don't. They also locate nonfiction books using the online catalog and note the call numbers of those books. Then the media specialist shows them how to access the CD-ROM encyclopedias and the Internet. She shows them where and how to type in their search terms. Again, some of the students find information on the CD-ROM, and some find useful information on the Internet.

When the students return to the library media center the next day, they work with fellow classmates on refining their search terms so that they can find information on the Internet. They get quite a few "hits," but some of them look like sites that want to sell items. They talk with the library media specialist about this and talk about information on the Internet—what is good, what is bad, and what is just plain incorrect.

Art

In art class, the students watch the movies on Chinese art: *Chinese Brush Painting* and *Heart of the Dragon*. They discuss the techniques used in creating Chinese brush art and talk about dragons, specifically Chinese dragons. They then create their own Chinese brush-art painting, trying to re-create a dragon. They review books with pictures of dragons in them, and the teacher reads to them about the history of dragons in Chinese art from the book *Dragons, Unicorns & Other Magical Beasts*.

In their next lesson, they create 3-D sculptures of dragons. An accordion-fold dragon is made out of construction paper. Large pieces of paper are folded for the body, and smaller pieces are used to create the legs. The head is made to look like a paper hat and then folded in half to make the head. This technique allows students to manipulate the head and open and shut the mouth. The teacher demonstrates how to glue the legs, head, and teeth and shows how to cut eyes, horns, teeth, etc. The students do this and then string the parts together to hang from the ceiling. The students use folding and symmetrical-cutting and cutting-multiples skills. The art teacher also introduces new vocabulary, such as *3-D*, *sculpture*, and *marionette*.

In the last lesson, the students use a large piece of either yellow, orange, or red 36-inch-wide bulletin-board paper on which to create a Chinese brush painting. Before they start painting, they glue a piece of basket reed in the form of a large circle to the back of the paper. When the painting is complete and dry, the students trim around the edges of the reed so that everyone has a large circle with a Chinese painting on one side. They finish their creations with tassel streamers tied to each side of the circle. The students will then learn from the music teacher how to move in a snake-like movement, and they will have a "dragon parade" during the next PTSA meeting.

Music

Students in music class experience the magical and exotic sounds of the Orient through song, instrument playing, and creative movement. To introduce the unit, fourth- and fifth-graders learn a song from Inner Mongolia called "Mongolian Night Song." Students discuss the differences between traditional American music and the sounds and instruments heard in the selection. They discuss what instruments in the classroom can be used to reproduce the sounds heard in the song. Metals, including metallophones, triangles, cymbals, and wind chimes, are selected. They learn rhythms that are comparative to the selection and transfer to the assorted pitched and unpitched instruments. The lesson requires about three weeks to complete. In following lessons, students learn about the Chinese Lion Dance and the drum and cymbal parts that are an integral part of the dance. The Lion moves throughout the streets of China to specific rhythms played by drums and cymbals during festivities such as Chinese New Year or the opening of a new business. When a new business is opened, the Lion visits the store and performs his dance. The store owner places a lettuce head, which represents the vegetable of longevity, in front of the store. The Lion begins his dance to a drum roll. He awakens, moves his head from right to left, looking for evil spirits. The cymbal begins to play a very loud, rhythmic pattern. The Lion moves from side to side, scaring off any evil spirits. When he spies the vegetable of longevity, the drum and cymbal play together and the Lion approaches the vegetable in a cat-and-mouse-type movement. He bites the vegetable, shakes his head, and spits it out, because it is very bitter. This symbolic gesture is supposed to bring good luck to the store owner. Many students experiment with the various drum and cymbal rhythms while other students move in response to the different sounds created by the drums and cymbals.

In later lessons, the students combine all rhythms, movements, and instruments with the Chinese streamers to perform an oriental piece.

P.E.

In P.E., the students study games played by Chinese children. Chinese jump rope is similar to American jump rope. They begin by jumping four times over each side of the rope and land with the rope between their legs. They then jump in with their feet together between two ropes, then jump out with both feet apart on the outside of both ropes, jump up, then crisscross their feet twice, and finally jump and land with each foot on each rope. The count is 1-2-3-4, in, out, crisscross, on the ropes, and so forth.

In the second game, students learn to move in ribbon movement to Chinese music. They first circle to the side, then circle overhead. Then the dancers do a figure eight, wave their ribbons, and then start walking while waving the ribbons.

These movements are more dance-like in nature and are used during the dragon parade, which is to be performed for the PTSA.

Evaluation

Classroom

Excellent

- Student has participated completely in class activities.

- Student has demonstrated interest by further pursuing information outside the classroom and has shared that information with classmates.

- Student has written a concise, clear report with interesting facts about the topic.

- Student presents the oral report creatively and demonstrates knowledge of the topic.

Adequate

- Student has participated some in class activities.

- Student has completed research on his or her topic.

- Student has created a report that is correct with only a few grammatical and content errors.

- Student presents report that is adequate but not particularly creative.

Inadequate

- Student has not participated.

- Student has not completed research adequately.

- Student's report contains errors in grammar and content.

- Student's oral report is not properly prepared.

Art

Excellent

- Student has participated fully in creating brush-art painting and the 3-D dragon.

- Student has created an exceptional piece of artwork.

Adequate

- Student has participated with minimal help in creating artwork.

Inadequate

- Student has failed to participate in creating artwork.

Music

Excellent

- Student has listened carefully to history of music and dance in China.

- Student has volunteered to play an instrument or dance in the parade.

- Student has grasped concepts of Chinese rhythm and melody.

- Student will perform in the parade for PTSA.

Adequate

- Student has learned to play an instrument or dance with coaxing and coaching.

- Student has understood most of the rhythm and melody patterns in Chinese music.

- Student has reluctantly agreed to perform in the parade for the PTSA.

Inadequate

- Student has not participated in class discussions.

- Student has not been able to understand rhythm or melody concepts or patterns.

- Student has not been able to replicate sounds on the Orff instruments.

- Student refuses to participate in parade for PTSA.

P.E.

Excellent

- Student has participated in games.

- Student learned the concepts quickly and performs them proficiently.

From *Fostering Information Literacy: Connecting National Standards, Goals 2000, and the SCANS Report.* © 2000 Libraries Unlimited. (800) 237-6124.

Adequate

- Student has participated most of the time.

- Student shows adequate proficiency in playing the games.

Inadequate

- Student rarely participates.

- Student does not demonstrate ability to understand game concepts or ability to play them.

Follow-up Activity

When the dragon parade is performed for the PTSA, the music teacher will have the students carry their circular paintings, which were created in art class, and move down the hall into the auditorium (while some students play the barred Orff xylophones and metallophones). When the parade reaches the stage, some students will perform the Lion Dance with drums and cymbals. Also, some students will wave streamers to represent the firecrackers shot off during a traditional Chinese parade.

SAMPLE INTEGRATED
LESSON PLAN III—FROGS

Grade Level 3: Needs Assessment

National Science Standard C states:

1. Students should understand the characteristics of organisms.

2. Students should understand the life cycle of organisms.

3. Students should understand the environments necessary for survival and the relationship between organisms and their environments.

After giving the third-graders a pre-test on frogs with questions about their life cycle, food requirements, and the environments they live in, it became clear that most of the students lacked fundamental information about the subject.

Background Information

Ms. McKinney, a third-grade teacher, started a terrarium environment in her classroom. She wanted to produce an ecosystem that would sustain frog life, show frog reproduction, and demonstrate the stages of life from egg to frog. The students were going to investigate what the frogs ate and what the environment should look like as far as water, temperature, and plants. Hopefully, the environment they created would produce eggs. If this happened, then the students would track the length of gestation of the eggs, how many tadpoles were reproduced, the changes in the tadpoles as they grew, and how long that process—from egg to full growth—would take.

Goals and Objectives

Science Goals

1. The students will understand the life cycle of the frog.

2. The students will understand the relationship between the organism and its environment.

3. The students will use data to construct simple investigations.

Science Objectives

1. The students will be able to chart the progress of frog life from egg to adult.

2.   The students will be able to explain the interrelationship of the frog and its environment.

3.   The students will be able to compare what they knew to what they learn based on their data collection and observations of the frog environment.

Information Literacy Goals

1.   Students will use the information they discover effectively.

2.   Students will work in groups collaboratively in collecting data.

3.   Students will work for excellence in gathering information.

Information Literacy Objectives

1.   Students will be able to organize the information they gather and apply that information in seeking answers to their questions.

2.   Students will be able to share information with others and collectively produce a complete picture of frog life.

3.   Students will be able to assess what they have learned and apply that knowledge in other areas.

Responsibilities

Classroom Teacher

1.   The teacher will introduce the subject and provide posters showing the frog life cycle.

2.   The teacher will provide the resources to build the terrarium environment.

3.   The teacher will lead the groups in the research process so that they can discover for themselves the necessary plants, temperature, and water content necessary to sustain frog life.

4.   The teacher will supervise the "building" of the environment.

Library Media Specialist

1.   The library media specialist will provide resources for the students to research.

2.   The library media specialist will work with small groups in the library media center in researching frogs and their environments.

3.   The library media specialist will act as a resource in finding plants and animals in the community.

Resources and Materials

Reference materials on frogs including texts, CD-ROMs, and Internet access

Posters on frog life cycle

Terrarium

Plants

Thermometer, heater, pump

Frogs

Frog food

Charts for plotting data collected

Journal for each student for keeping data information

Activities

The students must first be introduced to the unit. The teacher does this by explaining the frog life cycle and showing the poster illustration. The class then brainstorms what an animal needs to survive—food, temperature control, etc. She then has the students write down a list of items necessary to sustain life. The class talks about what kind of frog they will study, which will be a common frog that is indigenous to their area. The class then goes to the library media center where the library media specialist has pulled some resources for the class to look at. The teacher then breaks the class into groups and each group researches a specific topic as follows:

Group 1—food sources

Group 2—plants in the environment

Group 3—water needs and temperature needs

Group 4—life cycle—length, stages, etc.

The groups will come to the library media center as many times as necessary to gather their information, and the library media specialist will work with them in small groups.

Once all their information has been gathered, the library media specialist and the teacher will work on gathering the necessary plants, food, frogs, etc. needed to set up the terrarium.

Once the resources have been gathered, the class must work together in creating the terrarium's environment: how much dirt or gravel needs to be used, how many ponds or water sources to have, where plants need to go, etc. They will also need to have a feeding schedule for the frogs and assign responsibility to each group for feeding.

After the terrarium has been established, the class will also have to assign a rotating schedule for each group to check the terrarium for signs of eggs. If they are lucky and eggs are produced, they will need to continue the schedule to observe the gestation of the eggs and each stage thereafter. Each group will need to assign a recorder to record data, dates, time, etc. Each group will then contribute information on their topic and the class will produce one finished project based on the data they collected.

Evaluation

Excellent

- The student participated fully in his or her group; the evaluation is based on the participation of all the other members of the group.

- The student was responsible in fulfilling the duties of observer, recorder, feeder, etc.

- The student contributed information for the finished product.

- The student scored a ninety or better on a post-test on frog life.

Adequate

- The student participated according to evaluation of most of the group.

- The student fulfilled his or her role most of the time in observing, recording, or feeding.

- The student contributed some information for the finished product.

- The student scored a seventy-five or better on a post-test.

Inadequate

- The student did not participate in comparison to the participation of other group members.

- The student did not fulfill his or her obligations in recording, feeding, or observing.

- The student did not contribute information for the final product.

- The student scored below a seventy-five on a post-test.

SAMPLE INTEGRATED
LESSON PLAN IV—HALLOWEEN

Grade Level 1: Needs Assessment

The National Math Standards state:

1. Students should understand how mathematics relates to physical materials, pictures, and diagrams.

2. Students should understand whole-number concepts and skills.

3. Students should experience data analysis and probability.

The National Standards for English Language Arts state:

1. Students should apply knowledge of language structure and conventions.

2. Students should employ a wide range of strategies as they write.

These students are just starting on their educational voyage and have no concept of charts or graphs or of the different parts of speech and their labels.

Background Information

This lesson is just in time for Halloween. To tie in everyday objects and holiday occurrences with math and English concepts, the first-grade teachers have decided to use candy gathered during trick-or-treating to show charting and whole-number, sorting, and counting strategies. They have also decided to use the pumpkins each student picked on a field trip to the pumpkin patch to illustrate the use of adjectives and to take advantage of the opportunity for a creative writing activity.

Goals and Objectives

Math Goals

1. Students will relate a physical item to a mathematical concept.

2. Students will understand whole-number concepts.

3. Students will understand data collection and analysis.

From *Fostering Information Literacy: Connecting National Standards, Goals 2000, and the SCANS Report.* © 2000 Libraries Unlimited. (800) 237-6124.

Math Objectives

1. Students will be able to plot their candy collection on a chart.

2. Students will be able to count and group their candy.

3. Students will be able to organize and describe their candy in chart form.

Language Arts Goals

1. Students will understand a part of speech.

2. Students will understand the relation of that part of speech in writing.

Language Arts Objectives

1. Student will be able to describe the pumpkin face by using an adjective.

2. Student will be able to write a short paragraph about the pumpkin and use the adjective in the paragraph.

Information Literacy Goals

Students will use the information they gather effectively.

Information Literacy Objectives

1. Students will be able to organize the information they gather for practical application.

2. Students will incorporate new information about charting and language application into their own knowledge bank.

3. Students will be able to apply information gathered in problem solving.

Responsibilities

Classroom Teacher

1. The teacher will introduce the concept of charts and practice counting, collecting, organizing, and charting various items—paper shapes, different dried beans, pasta shapes.

2. The teacher will discuss the parts of speech and focus on adjectives.

Resources and Materials

Charts

Beans, pasta, paper shapes

Pictures of faces with various expressions

Activities

Math

The students focus on charting in math. The teacher brings in various items and has the students collect, organize, and sort the items. For instance, she has brought in various kinds of dried beans. The students have to pick through the beans and put like beans together—black beans, kidney beans, lima beans, etc. She then introduces a bar chart and shows the students how numbers are lined up vertically with the bean categories lined up horizontally. She can introduce the vocabulary of x-axis and y-axis and discuss how those terms relate to the chart. She then has the students count the various numbers of each type of bean and shows how that information is plotted on the chart. The class can then assess which type of bean they have the most of and which they have the least of, etc.

Language Arts

In language arts, the students are learning about parts of speech. They are focusing on adjectives. The teacher talks about what adjectives are and how they describe something. They then play a guessing game in class. The teacher picks something in the class and gives clues to what it is in response to students' questions. They must ask a question using an adjective—is it big, small, square, pink, blue, etc. The teacher writes the correct "adjective clues" on the board until a description emerges that allows the students to guess what the object is. She also plays another game with them: She holds up pictures of different faces showing different expressions; the students then describe what they see. The students also write short stories about the objects found in the guessing game and the faces they have seen and described.

As a tie-in with Halloween, the students will take home a graph showing the various types of candy they might receive on Halloween. They will have to sort, count, and graph their candy.

In addition, each student will have to carve a pumpkin face and describe whether the face is happy, mean, sad, etc. They will then each write a short paragraph about their pumpkins using the adjectives they chose to describe them.

Evaluation

Math

Excellent

- The student graphed his or her candy correctly, showing understanding of the concept.

Adequate

- The student graphed most of his or her candy correctly.

Inadequate

- The student did not graph his or her candy correctly and did not grasp the concept of sorting, counting, and organizing.

Language Arts

Excellent

- The student used a meaningful adjective to describe his or her pumpkin.

- The student wrote a paragraph about his or her pumpkin with correct grammar and spelling.

Adequate

- The student used a good adjective to describe his or her pumpkin.

- The student wrote a paragraph about his or her pumpkin with minor grammar and spelling mistakes.

Inadequate

- The student did not use an adjective to describe his or her pumpkin.

- The student failed to write a paragraph or wrote one with numerous grammatical and spelling errors.

NOTES

1.   Barbara K. Stripling and Judy M. Pitts, *Brainstorms and Blueprints: Teaching Library Research as a Thinking Process* (Englewood, CO: Libraries Unlimited, 1988), 53. This book introduces the concept of research as a thinking process by discussing the taxonomy of thoughtful research and the taxonomy of thoughtful reactions to research. Included with the book are numerous handouts to guide students in the research process.

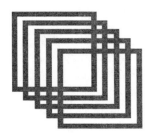

Chapter **10**

World Wide Web Resources

But desire of knowledge, like the thirst of riches,
increases ever with the acquisition of it.

—Laurence Sterne

The following links to Internet resources are provided in an effort to quench teachers' and library media specialists' thirst for more knowledge about information literacy. But, we hope their thirst will continue to increase as they desire even more knowledge and understanding.

INFORMATION LITERACY INTERNET RESOURCES

Barron, Daniel D. 1998. *Dan's Home Page.* URL: http://www.libsci.sc.edu/dan/dan.htm. Accessed November 8, 1999. Dr. Barron's Web site includes PowerPoint presentations about information literacy, and links to other information literacy sites. Click on "Courses I Like to Teach" and check out the resources in Taming the Information Technology Jungle and Educational Functions of Libraries.

Darrow, Rob. 1998. *Computer and Information Literacy Skills.* URL: http://www.schoollibrary. org/dhs/infolit.html. Accessed November 8, 1999. Sponsored by the California School Library Association, this site gives background information on information literacy and provides links to Information Literacy Frameworks sites, and sites on research about information literacy.

Educational Resources Information Center. 1994. *Information Literacy in an Information Society*. URL: http://www.ed.gov/databases/ERIC_Digests/ed372756.html. Accessed November 8, 1999. This ERIC Digest article was adapted from the document of the same title by Christina Doyle. It includes a definition of information literacy and Doyle's characteristics of an information-literate person. In addition, it gives the background of the information literacy movement, relates it to the SCANS Report and GOALS 2000, and considers the impact technology adds to the need for information literacy instruction. The article concludes with a call for educational reform and outlines the steps already taken by the developers of national curriculum standards.

Garland, Ken. 1998. *Librarians Information Online Network*. URL: http://www.libertynet.org/lion/lion.html. Accessed November 8, 1999. Connected with the School District of Philadelphia, this site has many valuable links for library media specialists. The ones related to this book are labeled "Issues in School Librarianship," "Forums," and "Lesson Plans."

Gay, Greg. 1998. *Learning to Learn: Thinking and Learning Skills*. URL: http://snow.utoronto.ca/Learn2/introll.html. Accessed November 8, 1999. This is an online course in learning how to learn. Topics covered in the interactive course are Consciousness, Metacognition, Learning Styles, Memory, Language, Reading, Problem Solving, Creativity, and Biology. Registration (free) is requested, but some parts are available without registering.

Hancock, Vicki E. 1993. *Information Literacy for Lifelong Learning*. URL: http://www.ed.gov/databases/ERIC.Digests/ed358870.html. Accessed November 8, 1999. This article explains the necessity of information literacy to meet the challenges of the Information Age and discusses the changes in the roles of teachers, library media specialists, and students. The author states that students who are involved in information literacy activities "seek a rich range of information sources; communicate an understanding of content; pose questions about the content being learned; use the environment, people, and tools for learning; reflect on their own learning; assess their own learning; and take responsibility for their own learning."

Johnston, Jerome. 1997. *Library User Information on the World Wide Web*. URL: http://www-personal.umich.edu/~kschwart/ed601/bibliography.htm. Accessed November 8, 1999. Part of Professor Johnston's Web site for an instructional design course, this page offers a bibliography of sites and resources related to library users and information literacy.

Maine Educational Media Association. 1997. *Information Literacy Projects*. URL: http://www.umcs.maine.edu/~orono/collaborative/collaborative.html. Accessed November 8, 1999. This listing of literature-based activities was developed by Maine teachers and librarians. The activities use the state's student book award nominees and incorporate information literacy skills in each unit.

Maine Educational Media Association Information Skills Committee. 1997. *SPRINGBOARD: Innovative Assessment of Electronic and Information Literacy*. URL: http://www.umcs.maine.edu/~orono/collaborative/spring/contents.html.

Accessed November 8, 1999. This site offers links to additional resources on information literacy and electronic literacy. Some of the sites contain information on assessment, portfolios, charts and use of Bloom's Taxonomy, national standards, and rubrics.

Miller, Elizabeth. 1998. *Elizabeth Miller*. URL: http://www.libsci.sc.edu/miller/elizabeth. htm. Accessed November 8, 1999. Elizabeth Miller, author of *Internet Resources for K–12 Educators*, has many valuable resources on her own Web site. Her *Conference Presentations* (including information on *Integrating Internet Resources into the Curriculum*), *Lesson Plans*, and *Library Links—Technology* are excellent for teachers and library media specialists.

Ontario Ministry of Education and Training. 1996. *Ontario's Information Literacy and Equitable Access: A Framework for Change and the Library Information Centre.* URL: http://www.tbe.edu/lib/model/other/other1.html. Accessed November 8, 1999. This article contains a synopsis of the document *Information Literacy and Equitable Access: A Framework for Change* and its impact on the role of teacher-librarians, especially in the area of equal access to information. The document defines information literacy as "the ability to acquire, critically evaluate, select, use, create, and communicate information in ways that lead to knowledge and wisdom." Its importance to students stems, in part, from its relationship to lifelong learning. Ontario's Ministry of Education and Training believes "guaranteeing equity of access to information, information skills, and information technology . . . remove[s] barriers—economic and others—to students realizing their potential." School libraries are envisioned as "evolving from collection-based facilities services to access-based services" where they "manage and provide information to students and teachers in classrooms and, when possible, in homes."

Oregon Educational Media Association. n.d. *Information Literacy Standards for Student Learning.* URL: http://www.teleport.com/~oema/infostd.html. Accessed November 8, 1999. This site lists the AECT/AASL information literacy standards and indicators.

Schrock, Kathleen. 1999. *Kathy Schrock's Guide for Educators—Critical Evaluation Surveys.* URL: http://school.discovery.com/schrockguide/eval.html. Accessed November 8, 1999. Kathy Schrock's critical evaluation page provides links to resource evaluation surveys developed for elementary, middle, and secondary school students and to other information on critical evaluation of Internet resources.

Swanson, Judy. 1998. *Information Competence: IC Sites on the Web.* URL: http://www. lib.calpoly.edu/infocomp/related.html. Accessed November 8, 1999. Sponsored by the California State University System, this site has links to information literacy background reports and projects and online tutorials and courses.

T.A.R.G.E.T. 1995. *LIBRARY: JK–Grade 9—A Diagram of the Library Information Model.* URL: http://www.tbe.edu/lib/model/curriculum/curr2.html#PIC. Accessed November 8, 1999. This site contains an interesting graphical representation of the Library Information Model. The model is divided into four overall segments: Learning Sources, Learning Resources, Learning Technologies, and Learning Partnerships. The Inquiring Student is in the center of the graphic and is circled by the information literacy activities of Accessing, Evaluating, Managing, and Using. Each segment may be clicked on to learn more about it.

T.A.R.G.E.T. 1996. *Library Models*. URL: http://www.tbe.edu/lib/model/model.html. Accessed November 8, 1999. Also from Toronto, this site contains links to "theoretical models of teaching and learning in the Library Information Centre."

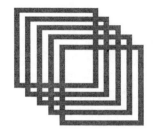

Afterword

Long ago, when I had my Merlyn to help,
he tried to teach me to think.
He knew he would have to leave in the end,
so he forced me to think for myself.

—*King Arthur* from
The Once and Future King
by T. H. White

LESSONS FROM MERLYN:
A MODEL FOR INFORMATION LITERACY
INSTRUCTION

They say a photographer sees the world through a camera's viewfinder. Every scene becomes a composition of form and color. The same is true of educators. Once you begin to think in terms of information literacy, illustrations of it can be found everywhere—in literature, in the movies, and in life itself. Some of my favorite examples of information literacy instruction are from *The Once and Future King* by T. H. White.[1] This fantasy novel tells the story of Wart, the future King Arthur, and his magical tutor, Merlyn. Merlyn's task was to prepare his student for the future—the same task we face today. Merlyn achieved this task by teaching the Wart to *think*—to become information literate. Merlyn's methods were creative and "hands-on" and revolved around real-life problem-solving situations. Granted, Merlyn was a magician, and that helped tremendously, but even though we are not magicians, we still can learn many lessons about fostering information literacy from Merlyn and his methods of instruction.

159

In the story, Sir Ector was responsible for seeing that his son, Kay, and his foster son, Wart, received an education. Sir Ector's idea of a "first rate eddication" included Latin, Repetition, Astrology, Archery, Tilting, and Horsemanship. His son, Kay, would grow up to be a knight and the Wart would grow up to be Sir Kay's squire; everyone knew that. The boys' educations would prepare them for their predictable futures, but Merlyn, who tutored them both, lived backwards and had the advantage of knowing the future is not always what it is predicted to be. He, and only he, knew that someday the Wart would be king of a crazy, wild little corner of the world. In order to survive in his kingdom, the Wart would have to adapt to change. In order to tame his kingdom, he would have to bring about change. To do both, he would have to learn to think—to effectively use all the knowledge and information available to understand and control a given situation. Therefore, while Merlyn gave both boys a traditional "eddication," he also instilled in the future King Arthur the ability to think.

How does this relate to information literacy? What can we learn from observing Merlyn? We can learn two things—our first two lessons:

To foster information literacy skills and attitudes:

1. Respect and teach each student as if he will become king, even though he and the rest of the world believe he will become merely a squire.

2. Teach students to think for themselves; prepare them for unpredictable, changeable futures. The ability to think enables them not only to adapt to change but also to initiate it.

Merlyn taught the Wart to think by letting him experience the world from different viewpoints. He began Wart's education by magically changing him into a fish:

> " 'Oh, Merlyn,' the Wart cried, 'please come too.'
>
> 'For this once,' said a large and solemn tench beside his ear, 'I will come. But in future you will have to go by yourself. Education is experience, and the essence of experience is self-reliance.' " (46)

By imitation and with lots of encouragement, the Wart learned to swim like a fish, not like a boy. From this we learn . . .

To foster information literacy:

3. Supervise students closely in the beginning, modeling skills and offering encouragement. Later, loosen control and allow them to be self-reliant.

When the Wart could swim with ease, Merlyn took him to see the King of the Moat, Black Peter. Mr. P., as he was called, was a four-foot-long pike who "was remorseless, logical, pitiless, fearful, and bitter. He was to speak to the Wart about Power."

> "There is nothing," said the monarch, "except the power which you pretend to seek. . . . There is only power. Power is of the individual mind, but the mind's power is not enough. Power of the body decides everything in the end, and only Might is Right." (52)

Why did Merlyn want Wart to meet Mr. P.? Possibly because . . .

To foster information literacy and respect for intellectual freedom:

4. Expose students to thoughts and ideas that others express, even disagreeable ones. Only by showing students what *is*, can we empower them to change it to what *ought to be*.

The Wart's next experience came on a cold, rainy night. He had been in a foul mood all day and was finally sent off by Sir Ector to find his tutor:

> "I think I ought to have some eddication," said the Wart. "I can't think of anything to do."
>
> "You think that education is something which ought to be done when all else fails?" inquired Merlyn nastily, for he was in a bad mood, too.
>
> "Well," said the Wart, "some sorts of education."
>
> "Mine?" asked the magician with flashing eyes.
>
> "Oh, Merlyn," exclaimed the Wart without answering, "please give me something to do, because I feel so miserable. Nobody wants me for anything today, and I just don't know how to be sensible. It rains so."
>
> "You could learn to knit."
>
> "Could I go out and be something, a fish or anything like that?"

> "You have been a fish," said Merlyn. "Nobody with any
> go needs to do their education twice."
>
> "Well, could I be a bird?" (73–74)

The lessons from this are . . .

To foster information literacy and a love of learning:

5. Combat students' boredom and restlessness by giving them meaningful learning experiences.

6. Vary these experiences.

It was finally agreed that the Wart would become a merlin, sit in the mews for the night, and talk to the other hunting birds. "That is the way to learn, by listening to the experts." From these experts, the Wart learned that a bird's most important members are his feet and the first law of the foot is never to let go. He also learned he could withstand the ordeal they presented by staying calm and using his wits. (75–85)

This scene illustrates two important instructional objectives necessary for learning to think.

To foster information literacy and critical thinking:

7. Give students opportunities to interact with experts in different fields.

To foster information literacy and encourage pursuit of personal interests:

8. Give students opportunities to learn about themselves. Self-discovery is as important as factual knowledge.

For the Wart's next educational adventure, Merlyn changed him into an ant. The ants lived as impersonal robots who did not think or act on their own. Their lives were orderly, and predictable, but their thoughts and actions were not their own. Even their language was limited to "done" (good) and "not done" (bad):

> But we need not go on about the ants in too much detail—
> they are not a pleasant subject. It is enough to say that
> the boy went on living among them, conforming to
> their habits, watching them so as to understand as much

> as he could, but unable to ask questions. It was not only that their language had not got the words in which humans are interested . . . but also that it was dangerous to ask questions at all. A question was a sign of insanity to them. Their life was not questionable: It was dictated. (127–28)

To foster information literacy and promote the importance of information to a democratic society:

9.   Encourage and permit students to question.

The Wart learned to fly on another magical adventure. He spent an evening with Archimedes, Merlyn's wise and beloved owl. His first attempts at flying were nearly disastrous. He went up, then down, up again, then down. It was very tiring:

> "For heaven's sake," panted Archimedes, "stop flying like a woodpecker. . . . What you are doing is to give yourself flying speed with one flick of your wings. You then rise on that flick until you have lost flying speed and begin to stall. Then you give another just as you are beginning to drop out of the air, and do a switch-back. . . . Waver your wings all the time, like me, instead of doing these jumps with them."
>
> The Wart did what he was told, and was surprised to find that the earth became stable and moved underneath him without tilting, in a regular pour. He did not feel himself to be moving at all. (161–62)

The owl was a patient and attentive teacher. We can learn much from him.

To foster information literacy and confidence in learning:

10.   Do not expect perfection from a student's first attempts with a new concept or skill. Accept mistakes graciously and without undue criticism.

11.   Allow some assignments to be redone. At the same time, however, constantly and carefully observe and evaluate student performance. Timely intervention will encourage success and may avert failure.

> "Now that you have learned to fly," said Archimedes, "Merlyn wants you to try the Wild Geese." (164)

The Wart immediately found himself among a crowd of beautiful, wild White-fronted Geese. He watched and listened and imitated, and eventually joined in the joyous camaraderie of a migration across the North Sea. He became friends with a White-front named Lyo-lyok. When he confessed that he was really a human, sent for his education, she was only mildly surprised.

> "He grew fond of Lyo-lyok, in spite of her being a girl. He was always asking her questions about the geese. She taught him what she knew with gentle kindness, and the more he learned, the more he came to love her brave, noble, quiet and intelligent relations." (171)

Lyo-lyok was a wise and kind teacher also. From her we learn . . .

To foster information literacy and respect for others' ideas, backgrounds, and contributions:

12. Expose students to people who are different—intellectually, physically, or culturally. Answer their questions with gentle kindness and they will come to respect, appreciate, and value the differences.

On the day Kay was to be knighted, Sir Ector found the Wart sulking in the kitchen and sent him again to Merlyn:

> "Sir Ector has given me a glass of canary," said the Wart, "and sent me to see if you can't cheer me up."
>
> "Sir Ector," said Merlyn, "is a wise man. . . . The best thing for being sad is to learn something. That is the one thing that never fails. . . . Learn why the world wags and what wags it. That is the only thing which the mind can never exhaust, never alienate, never be tortured by, never fear or distrust, and never dream of regretting. Learning is the thing for you."
>
> "Apart from all these things," said the Wart, "what do you suggest for me just now?"

> "You had better meet my friend the badger. . . . Except for Archimedes, he is the most learned creature I know. You will like him."
>
> "By the way," added the magician, "there is one thing I ought to tell you. This is the last time I shall be able to turn you into anything. All the magic for that sort of thing has been used up, and this will be the end of your education. . . . Do you think you have learned anything?"
>
> "I have learned, and been happy." (182–83)

We teachers have great influence on our students. We teach by example, so . . .

To foster information literacy and an appreciation of learning:

13.   Share the joy and excitement of learning. Lifelong learners are happy people.

The Wart did like Badger, and admired his muscles, tight chest, and mighty forearms.

> "What enormous arms you have," remarked the Wart. . . . So have I, for that matter."
>
> "It is to dig with," said the learned creature complacently. "Now what could have possessed Merlyn to send you to me?"
>
> "He was talking about learning," said the Wart.
>
> "Ah, well, if it is learning you are after, you have come to the right shop. . . . I am writing a treatise just now . . . which is to point out why Man has become master of the animals. Perhaps you would like to hear it? . . . It will be good for you, dear boy. It is just the thing to top off an education. Study birds and fish and animals: then finish off with Man." (189–90)

The badger's treatise, which was for his doctor's degree, explained that when God finished creating the eggs from which all animals would emerge, He lined up the embryos in front of Him and announced that He was giving them a chance to alter a part of themselves into a useful tool. Some chose to use their arms as flying machines and their mouths as weapons or crackers. Others selected to use their bodies as boats and their hands as oars. Still others turned their skins into shields and their arms into garden forks. After two days, all the embryos had chosen their specializations, except Man.

> "Please God," said the embryo Man, "I think that You made me in the shape which I now have for reasons best known to Yourselves, and that it would be rude to change. If I am to have my choice I will stay as I am. I will not alter any of the parts which You gave me, for other and doubtless inferior tools, and I will stay a defenseless embryo all my life, doing my best to make myself a few feeble implements out of the wood, iron and the other materials which You have seen fit to put before me. . . ."
>
> "Well done," exclaimed the Creator in delighted tones. . . . "Here, all you embryos . . . look upon Our first Man. He is the only one who has guessed Our riddle . . . Man, you will be a naked tool all your life, though a user of tools. You will look like an embryo till they bury you, but all the others will be embryos before your might. Eternally undeveloped, you will always remain potential in Our image. . . ." (192–93)

Merlyn wanted to remind the Wart that only humans can think and reason. It would become his greatest strength. It will be our students' greatest strength as well, so . . .

To foster information literacy, thinking skills, and problem solving:

14. Challenge and encourage students to ponder. Remind them that human beings' power lies in their ability to think and to fashion the tools they need to succeed; their potential is unlimited.

Soon after Kay was knighted, King Uther died, leaving no known heir to the throne. There was, instead, a sword set in stone. It was said that the person who could pull the sword from the stone would become the rightful king. Since, so far, no one had been able to budge the sword, a tournament was held to decide who would be king. Sir Ector, Sir Kay, his squire Wart, and the rest of the household traveled to London. On the morning of the great tournament, Sir Kay forgot his sword and sent his squire back to the inn to fetch it. The inn was locked. The Wart rode desperately through the streets looking for a sword to borrow or steal to take back to Sir Kay. He had not heard the story about the sword in the stone, so when he happened upon it, he thought it was some sort of war memorial. At his first tug, nothing happened. He pulled again. Still nothing.

> "Oh Merlyn," cried the Wart, "help me to get this weapon."
>
> There was a kind of rushing noise, and a long chord played along with it. All round the churchyard there were hundreds of old friends. . . . They loomed round the church wall, the lovers and helpers of the Wart, and they all spoke solemnly in turn . . . all . . . had come to help on account of love. Wart felt his power grow.
>
> "Put your back into it," said a . . . pike. . . . "Remember that power springs from the nape of the neck."
>
> "What about those forearms," asked a Badger gravely. . . . "Come along, my dear embryo, and find your tool."
>
> A merlin sitting at the top of the yew tree cried out, "Now then, Captain Wart, what is the first law of the foot? I thought I once heard something about never letting go?"
>
> "Don't work like a stalling woodpecker," urged a Tawny Owl affectionately. "Keep up a steady effort, my duck, and you will have it yet."
>
> A White-front said, "Now, Wart, if you were once able to fly the great North Sea, surely you can co-ordinate a few little wing-muscles here and there? Fold your powers together, with the spirit of your mind, and it will come out like butter. Come along, Homo sapiens, for all we humble friends of yours are waiting here to cheer."
>
> The Wart walked up to the great sword for the third time. He put out his right hand softly and drew it out as gently as from a scabbard. (204–5)

This is perhaps the most important lesson we can learn from Merlyn. It is . . .

To foster information literacy:

15. Teach students the skills they need to overcome the hurdles they meet and support them with love. Then they will have the power to be successful.

The Wart's education did not truly end when Merlyn's magic ran out, nor when he became King. Merlyn, as all great teachers do, remained a mentor for several years—advising, encouraging, and supporting, but also forcing Arthur to think for himself. Merlyn taught the child, Wart, about the world and how it wagged. Now he encouraged the King, Arthur, to think about what was wrong with that wagging and how it could be improved. Arthur thought, and determined the notion "Might Is Right" was wrong. He thought some more and resolved to create the Knights of the Round Table and, later, to initiate the Quest for the Holy Grail. As a result of Merlyn's teaching and Arthur's thinking, that crazy, wild little corner of the world became—for a while—the peaceful, civilized, almost magical Kingdom of Camelot.

These lessons from Merlyn don't require a magician's magical wand. Even as mere mortals, we can use them to do the same for our students—to teach them to *think*——to become information literate, to understand their world and what wags it, to cope, to solve problems, and to bring about change if necessary. The world will be a better place if we do. Let's do it!

REFERENCES

1. T. H. White, *The Once and Future King*, Ace Edition (New York: G. P. Putnam's Sons, 1987).

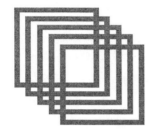

Appendix A: National Math Standards

The following chart compares the K–4 National Math Standards to the AASL/AECT Information Literacy Standards for Student Learning. Each math standard on the left side of the chart corresponds to the information literacy standard(s) and indicator(s) aligned on the right. There are three types of relationships depicted in the chart: 1) the information literacy standard or indicator *is similar* to the content standard, 2) the information literacy standard or indicator *is necessary to master* the content standard, or 3) the content standard and the information literacy standard(s) or indicator(s) *will be achieved using the same teaching practices*. While the most obvious indicators are listed, there are certainly others that may apply.

This comparison chart may be used in conjunction with the Checklist of Information Literacy Goals, Objectives, and Strategies found in chapter 8. Together the chart and the checklist become valuable tools for planning units and lessons that integrate information literacy skills into the subject-area curriculum.

The math standards are reprinted with permission from *Curriculum and Evaluation Standards for School Mathematics*, copyright 1989 by the National Council of Teachers of Mathematics. All rights reserved.

The AASL/AECT Information Literacy Standards are from *Information Power: Building Partnerships for Learning* by American Association of School Libraries and Association for Educational Communications and Technology. Copyright © 1998 American Library Association and Association for Educational Communications and Technology. Reprinted by permission of the American Library Association.

STANDARD 1: MATHEMATICS AS PROBLEM SOLVING

MATH STANDARDS K-4

The study of mathematics should emphasize problem solving so that students can:

AASL/AECT INFORMATION LITERACY STANDARDS

Information-literate students can:

- Use problem-solving approaches to investigate and understand mathematical content

- Apply information in critical thinking and problem solving (3.3)

- Formulate problems from everyday and mathematical situations

- Formulate questions based on information needs (1.3)

- Develop and apply strategies to solve a wide variety of problems

- Devise strategies for revising, improving, and updating self-generated knowledge (6.2)

- Verify and interpret results with respect to the original problems

- Determine accuracy, relevance, and comprehensiveness (2.1)

- Acquire confidence in using mathematics meaningfully

- Integrate new information into one's own knowledge (3.2)

STANDARD 2: MATHEMATICS AS COMMUNICATION

MATH STANDARDS K-4

The study of mathematics should include numerous opportunities for communication so that students can:

AASL/AECT INFORMATION LITERACY STANDARDS

Information-literate students can:

- Relate physical materials, pictures, and diagrams to mathematical ideas

- Derive meaning from information presented creatively in a variety of formats (5.2)

- Reflect on and clarify their thinking about mathematical ideas and situations

- Organize information for practical applications (3.1)

- Relate their everyday language to mathematical language and symbols

- Realize that representing, discussing, reading, writing, and listening to mathematics are a vital part of learning and using mathematics

- Integrate new information into one's own knowledge (3.2)

- Apply information in critical thinking and problem solving (3.3);
- Produce and communicate information and ideas in appropriate formats (3.4);
- Seek information related to personal interests (4.0)

STANDARD 3: MATHEMATICS AS REASONING

MATH STANDARDS K-4	AASL/AECT INFORMATION LITERACY STANDARDS
The study of mathematics should emphasize reasoning so that students can:	**Information-literate students can:**
• Draw logical conclusions about mathematics	• Apply information in critical thinking and problem solving (3.3)
• Use models, known facts, properties, and relationships to explain their thinking	• Produce and communicate information and ideas in appropriate formats (3.4)
• Justify their answers and their solutions processes	• Determine accuracy, relevance, and comprehensiveness (2.1); • Assess the quality of the process and products of personal information seeking (6.1)
• Use patterns and relationships to analyze mathematical situations	• Derive meaning from information presented creatively in a variety of formats (5.2)
• Believe that mathematics makes sense	• Integrate information into one's own knowledge (3.2); • Apply information in critical thinking and problem solving (3.3)

STANDARD 4: MATHEMATICAL CONNECTIONS

MATH STANDARDS K-4	AASL/AECT INFORMATION LITERACY STANDARDS
The study of mathematics should include opportunities to make connections so that students can:	Information-literate students can:
• Link conceptual and procedural knowledge	• Apply information in critical thinking and problem solving (3.3)
• Relate various representatives of concepts or procedures to one another	• Select information appropriate to the problem or question at hand (2.4)
• Recognize relationships among different topics in mathematics	• Evaluate information critically and competently (2.0)
• Use mathematics in other curriculum areas	• Apply information in critical thinking and problem solving (3.3)
• Use mathematics in their daily lives	• Seek information related to various dimensions of personal well-being (4.1); • Design, develop, and evaluate information products and solutions related to personal interests (4.2)

STANDARD 5: ESTIMATION

MATH STANDARDS K-4	AASL/AECT INFORMATION LITERACY STANDARDS
The curriculum should include estimation so students can:	Information-literate students can:
• Explore estimation strategies	• Develop and use successful strategies for locating information (1.5)
• Recognize when an estimate is appropriate	• Select information appropriate to the problem or question at hand (2.4)

- Determine the reasonableness of results

- Determine accuracy, relevance, and comprehensiveness (2.1)

- Apply estimation in working with quantities, measurement, computation, and problem solving

- Apply information in critical thinking and problem solving (3.3)

STANDARD 6: NUMBER SENSE AND NUMERATION

MATH STANDARDS K-4	**AASL/AECT INFORMATION LITERACY STANDARDS**
The mathematics curriculum should include whole-number concepts and skills so that students can:	**Information-literate students can:**
• Construct number meanings through real-world experiences and the use of physical materials	• Derive meaning from information in a variety of formats (5.2)
• Understand our numeration system by relating counting, grouping, and place-value concepts	• Organize information for practical applications (3.1)
• Develop number sense	• Integrate new information into one's own knowledge (3.2)
• Interpret the multiple uses of numbers encountered in the real world	• Derive meaning from information presented creatively in a variety of formats (5.2)

STANDARD 7: CONCEPTS OF WHOLE-NUMBER OPERATIONS

MATH STANDARDS K-4	AASL/AECT INFORMATION LITERACY STANDARDS
The mathematics curriculum should include concepts of addition, subtraction, multiplication, and division of whole numbers so that students can:	Information-literate students can:
• Develop meaning for the operations by modeling and discussing a rich variety of problem situations	• Share knowledge and information with others (9.1); • Collaborate with others to identify problems and to seek their solutions (9.3)
• Relate the mathematical language and symbolism of operations to problem solutions and informal language	• Select information appropriate to the problem or question at hand (2.4)
• Recognize that a wide variety of problem structures can be represented by a single operation	• Organize information for practical applications (3.1)
• Develop operation sense	• Integrate new information into one's own knowledge (3.2)

STANDARD 8: WHOLE-NUMBER COMPUTATION

MATH STANDARDS K-4	AASL/AECT INFORMATION LITERACY STANDARDS
The mathematics curriculum should develop whole-number computation so that students can:	Information-literate students can:
• Model, explain, and develop reasonable proficiency with basic facts and algorithms	• Produce and communicate information in appropriate formats (3.4)
• Use a variety of mental computation and estimation techniques	• Select information appropriate to the problem at hand (2.4)

- Use calculators in appropriate computational situations

- Use information technology responsibly (8.3)

- Select and use computation techniques appropriate to specific problems and determine whether the results are reasonable

- Formulate questions based on information needs (1.3);
- Apply information in critical thinking and problem solving (3.3);
- Assess the quality of the process and products of personal information seeking (6.1)

STANDARD 9: GEOMETRY AND SPATIAL SENSE

MATH STANDARDS K-4	AASL/AECT INFORMATION LITERACY STANDARDS
The mathematics curriculum should include two- and three-dimensional geometry so that students can:	**Information-literate students can:**
• Describe, model, draw, and classify shapes	• Derive meaning from information presented in a variety of formats (5.2); • Produce and communicate information and ideas in appropriate formats (3.1); • Organize information for practical applications (3.1)
• Investigate and predict the results of combining, subdividing, and changing shapes	• Apply information in critical thinking and problem solving (3.3)
• Develop spatial sense	• Integrate new information into one's own knowledge (3.2)
• Relate geometric ideas to number and measurement ideas	• Integrate new information into one's own knowledge (3.2)
• Recognize and appreciate geometry in their world	• Appreciate creative expressions of information (5.0)

STANDARD 10: MEASUREMENT

MATH STANDARDS K-4	AASL/AECT INFORMATION LITERACY STANDARDS
The mathematics curriculum should include measurement so that students can:	Information-literate students can:
• Understand the attributes of length, capacity, weight, mass, area, volume, time, temperature, and angle	• Identify a variety of potential sources of information (1.4); • Derive meaning from information presented creatively in a variety of formats (5.2)
• Develop the process of measuring and concepts related to units of measurement	• Develop and use successful strategies for obtaining information (1.5)
• Make and use estimates of measurement	• Select information appropriate to the problem or question at hand (2.4)
• Make and use measurements in problems and everyday situations	• Apply information in critical thinking and problem solving (3.3)

STANDARD 11: STATISTICS AND PROBABILITY

MATH STANDARDS K-4	AASL/AECT INFORMATION LITERACY STANDARDS
The mathematics curriculum should include experiences with data analysis and probability so that students can:	Information-literate students can:
• Collect, organize, and describe data	• Develop and use successful strategies for locating information (1.5); • Organize information for practical application (3.1)
• Construct, read, and interpret displays of data	• Produce and communicate information and ideas in appropriate formats (3.4); • Derive meaning from information presented creatively in a variety of formats (5.2)

- Formulate and solve problems that involve collecting and analyzing data

- Formulate questions based on information needs (1.3);
- Organize information for practical applications (3.1);
- Apply information in critical thinking and problem solving (3.3)

- Explore concepts of chance

- Recognize the need for information (1.1)

STANDARD 12: FRACTIONS AND DECIMALS

MATH STANDARDS K-4	AASL/AECT INFORMATION LITERACY STANDARDS
The mathematics curriculum should include fractions and decimals so that students can:	**Information-literate students can:**
• Develop concepts of fractions, mixed numbers, and decimals	• Derive meaning from information presented creatively in a variety of formats (5.2)
• Develop number sense for fractions and decimals	• Integrate new information into one's own knowledge (3.2)
• Use models to relate fractions to decimals and to find equivalent fractions	• Produce and communicate information and ideas in appropriate formats (3.4)
• Use models to explore operations on fractions and decimals	• Derive meaning from information presented creatively in a variety of formats (5.2)
• Apply fractions and decimals to problem situations	• Apply information in critical thinking and problem solving (3.3)

STANDARD 13: PATTERNS AND RELATIONSHIPS

MATH STANDARDS K-4	AASL/AECT INFORMATION LITERACY STANDARDS
The mathematics curriculum should include the study of patterns and relationships so that students can:	**Information-literate students can:**
• Recognize, describe, extend, and create a wide variety of patterns	• Derive meaning from information in a variety of formats (5.2); • Develop creative products in a variety of formats (5.3)
• Represent and describe mathematical relationships	• Select information appropriate to the problem or question at hand (2.4)
• Explore the use of variables and open sentences to express relationships	• Apply information in critical thinking and problem solving (3.3); • Produce and communicate information and ideas in appropriate formats (3.4)

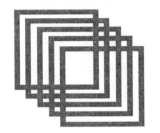

Appendix B: National Science Standards

The following chart compares the National Science Standards to the AASL/AECT Information Literacy Standards for Student Learning. Each science standard on the left side of the chart corresponds to the information literacy standard(s) and indicator(s) aligned on the right. There are three types of relationships depicted in the chart: 1) the information literacy standard or indicator *is similar* to the content standard, 2) the information literacy standard or indicator *is necessary to master* the content standard, or 3) the content standard and the information literacy standard(s) or indicator(s) *will be achieved using the same teaching practices*. While the most obvious indicators are listed, there are certainly others that may apply.

This comparison chart may be used in conjunction with the Checklist of Information Literacy Goals, Objectives, and Strategies found in chapter 8. Together the chart and the checklist become valuable tools for planning units and lessons that integrate information literacy skills into the subject-area curriculum.

The science standards are reprinted with permission from *National Science Education Standards*. Copyright 1995 by the National Academy of Sciences. Courtesy of the National Academy Press, Washington, DC.

The AASL/AECT Information Literacy Standards are from *Information Power: Building Partnerships for Learning* by American Association of School Libraries and Association for Educational Communications and Technology. Copyright © 1998 American Library Association and Association for Educational Communications and Technology. Reprinted by permission of the American Library Association.

CONTENT STANDARD A: SCIENCE AS INQUIRY

NATIONAL SCIENCE EDUCATION CONTENT STANDARDS K-4	AASL/AECT INFORMATION LITERACY STANDARDS
As a result of activities in grades K-4, all students should develop:	**Information-literate students can:**

Abilities necessary to do scientific inquiry so they can:

- Ask a question about objects, organisms, and events in the environment

  - Formulate questions based on information needs (1.3)

- Employ simple equipment and tools to gather data and extend the senses

  - Use information technology responsibly (8.3);
  - Derive meaning from information presented creatively in a variety of formats (5.2)

- Use data to construct a reasonable explanation

  - Select information appropriate to the problem or question at hand (2.4);
  - Apply information in critical thinking and problem solving (3.3)

- Communicate investigations and explanations

  - Share knowledge and information with others (9.1)

Understanding about scientific inquiry

- Scientific investigations involve asking and answering a question and comparing the answer with what scientists already know about the world.

  - Recognize the need for information (1.1);
  - Recognize that accurate and comprehensive information is the basis for intelligent decision making (1.2)

- Scientists use different kinds of investigations depending on the questions they are trying to answer. Types of investigations include describing objects, events, and organisms; classifying them; and doing a fair test (experimenting).

  - Formulate questions based on information needs (1.3);
  - Develop and use successful strategies for locating information (1.5)

- Simple instruments, such as magnifiers, thermometers, and rulers, provide more information than scientists obtain using only their senses.

- Use information technology responsibly (8.3);
- Derive meaning from information presented creatively in a variety of formats (5.2)

- Scientists develop explanations using observations (evidence) and what they already know about the world (scientific knowledge). Good explanations are based on evidence from investigations.

- Select information appropriate to the problem or question at hand (2.4);
- Determine accuracy, relevance, and comprehensiveness (2.1);
- Organize information for practical applications (3.1);
- Apply information in critical thinking and problem solving (3.3)

- Scientists make the results of their investigations public; they describe the investigations in ways that enable others to repeat the investigations.

- Share knowledge with others (9.1);
- Respect principle of equitable access to information (7.2)

- Scientists review and ask questions about the results of other scientists' work.

- Respect others' ideas and backgrounds and acknowledge their contributions (9.2);
- Collaborate with others to identify information problems and to seek their solutions (9.3);
- Collaborate with others to design, develop, and evaluate information products and solutions related to personal interests (4.2)

CONTENT STANDARD B: PHYSICAL SCIENCE

NATIONAL SCIENCE EDUCATION CONTENT STANDARDS K-4	AASL/AECT INFORMATION LITERACY STANDARDS
As a result of their activities in grades K-4, all students should develop an understanding of:	**Information-literate students can:**
Properties of objects and materials:	

- Objects have many observable properties. Those properties can be measured using tools such as rulers, balances, and thermometers.

- Objects are made of one or more materials. Objects can be described and sorted by the properties of those materials.

- Materials can exist in different states.

- Position and motion of objects

- Light, heat, electricity, and magnetism

- Develop and use successful strategies for locating information (1.5);
- Use information technology responsibly (8.3)

- Select information appropriate to the problem or question at hand (2.4);
- Organize information for practical applications (3.1)

- Derive meaning from information in a variety of formats (5.2);
- Integrate new information into one's own knowledge (3.2)

- Integrate new information into one's own knowledge (3.2)

- Integrate new information into one's own knowledge (3.2)

CONTENT STANDARD C: LIFE SCIENCE

NATIONAL SCIENCE EDUCATION CONTENT STANDARDS K-4	AASL/AECT INFORMATION LITERACY STANDARDS

As a result of their activities in grades K-4, all students should develop an understanding of:

- The characteristics of organisms

The Life Science and the Earth and Space Science Standards deal strictly with science content knowledge; therefore they do not resemble any of the AASL/AECT Information Literacy Standards. However, according to the National Science Education Program Standards and Teacher Standards, the instructional methods by which they should be presented and learned are very similar to those advocated for fostering information literacy instruction.

- Life cycles of organisms
- Organisms and environments

CONTENT STANDARD D: EARTH AND SPACE SCIENCE

NATIONAL SCIENCE EDUCATION CONTENT STANDARDS K-4

As a result of their activities in grades K-4, all students should develop an understanding of:

- Properties of earth materials

- Objects in the sky

- Changes in the earth and sky

CONTENT STANDARD E: SCIENCE AND TECHNOLOGY

NATIONAL SCIENCE EDUCATION CONTENT STANDARDS K-4	AASL/AECT INFORMATION LITERACY STANDARDS
As a result of their activities in grades K-4, all students should develop:	**Information-literate students can:**
Abilities to do technological design so they can:	
• Identify a simple problem	• Recognize the need for information (1.1); • Formulate questions based on information needs (1.3); • Select information appropriate to the problem or question at hand (2.4)
• Propose a solution	• Produce and communicate information and ideas in appropriate formats (3.4)
• Implement a proposed solution	• Apply information in critical thinking and problem solving (3.3)
• Evaluate a product or design	• Assess the quality of the process and products of personal information seeking (6.1)

- Communicate a problem, design, and solution

- Produce and communicate information and ideas in appropriate formats (3.4);
- Share knowledge and information with others (9.1)

Understanding about science and technology

- People have always had questions about their world. Science is one way of answering questions and explaining the natural world.

- Recognize that accurate and comprehensive information is the basis for intelligent decision making (1.2)

- People have always had problems and invented tools and techniques to solve problems.

- Apply information in critical thinking and problem solving (3.3);
- Use information technology responsibly (8.3)

- Scientists and engineers often work in teams with different individuals doing different things that contribute to the results.

- Collaborate with others to identify information problems and to seek their solutions (9.3)

- Women and men of all ages, backgrounds, and groups engage in a variety of scientific and technological work.

- Respect others' ideas and backgrounds and acknowledge their contributions (9.2)

- Tools help scientists make better observations, measurements, and equipment for investigations.

- Identify a variety of potential sources of information (1.4);
- Develop and use successful strategies for locating information (1.5);

Abilities to distinguish between natural objects and objects made by humans

- Apply information in critical thinking and problem solving (3.3)

CONTENT STANDARD F: SCIENCE IN PERSONAL AND SOCIAL PERSPECTIVES

NATIONAL SCIENCE EDUCATION CONTENT STANDARDS K-4	AASL/AECT INFORMATION LITERACY STANDARDS
As a result of their activities in grades K-4, all students should develop an understanding of:	**Information-literate students can:**
• Personal health	• Seek information related to various dimensions of personal well-being (4.1); • Design, develop, and evaluate information products and solutions related to personal interests (4.2)
• Characteristics and changes in population	• Organize information for practical applications (3.1)
• Types of resources	• Identify a variety of potential sources of information (1.4); • Develop and use successful strategies for locating information (1.5)
• Changes in environments	• Organize information for practical applications (3.1)
• Science and technology in local challenges	• Apply information in critical thinking and problem solving (3.3); • Use information technology responsibly (8.3)

CONTENT STANDARD G: HISTORY AND NATURE OF SCIENCE

NATIONAL SCIENCE EDUCATION CONTENT STANDARDS K-4	AASL/AECT INFORMATION LITERACY STANDARDS
As a result of their activities in grades K-4, all students should develop an understanding of:	**Information-literate students can:**
Science as a human endeavor	
• Science and technology have been practiced by people for a long time.	• Recognize the need for information (1.1); • Recognize that accurate and comprehensive information is the basis for intelligent decision making (1.2)
• Men and women have made a variety of contributions throughout the history of science and technology.	• Respect others' ideas and backgrounds and acknowledge their contributions (9.2)
• Although men and women using scientific inquiry have learned much about the objects, events, and phenomena in nature, much more remains to be understood. Science will never be finished.	• Devise strategies for revising, improving, and updating self-generated knowledge (6.2); • Collaborate with others to identify information problems and to seek their solutions (9.3)
• Many people choose science as a career and devote their entire lives to studying it. Many people derive great pleasure from doing science.	• Pursue information related to interests (4.0); • Strive for excellence in information seeking and knowledge generation (6.0); • Participate effectively in groups to pursue and generate knowledge (9.0)

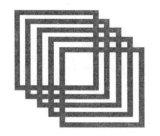

Appendix C:
National History
Standards

The following chart compares the National History Standards to the AASL/AECT Information Literacy Standards for Student Learning. Each history standard on the left side of the chart corresponds to the information literacy standard(s) and indicator(s) aligned on the right. There are three types of relationships depicted in the chart: 1) the information literacy standard or indicator *is similar* to the content standard, 2) the information literacy standard or indicator *is necessary to master* the content standard, or 3) the content standard and the information literacy standard(s) or indicator(s) *will be achieved using the same teaching practices*. While the most obvious indicators are listed, there are certainly others that may apply.

This comparison chart may be used in conjunction with the Checklist of Information Literacy Goals, Objectives, and Strategies found in chapter 8. Together the chart and the checklist become valuable tools for planning units and lessons that integrate information literacy skills into the subject-area curriculum.

The history standards are reprinted by permission of the National Center for History in the Schools at UCLA.

The AASL/AECT Information Literacy Standards are from *Information Power: Building Partnerships for Learning* by American Association of School Libraries and Association for Educational Communications and Technology. Copyright © 1998 American Library Association and Association for Educational Communications and Technology. Reprinted by permission of the American Library Association.

FAMILIES AND COMMUNITIES LONG AGO

NATIONAL HISTORY STANDARDS K-4	AASL/AECT INFORMATION LITERACY STANDARDS
Standard 1: Students should understand family life now and in the recent past and family life in various places long ago.	**Students should be able to demonstrate information literacy skills by:**
1A: Students should be able to demonstrate an understanding of family life now and in the past by:	

- Investigating a family history for at least two generations
- Identifying members and connections to prepare a timeline

- Drawing conclusions about roles in life from data gathered through photos

- Comparing and contrasting family life now with that of the past and between different cultures

- Examining and formulating questions about early records, etc. to describe family life in their state long ago

- Comparing and contrasting, through roles, family life now with family life in their state long ago

---

- Identifying a variety of potential sources of information (1.4);
- Organizing information for practical applications (3.1)

- Determining accuracy, relevancy, and comprehensiveness (2.1);
- Distinguishing among fact, point of view, and opinion (2.2)

- Applying information in critical thinking and problem solving (3.3)

- Formulating questions based on information needs (1.3);
- Identifying a variety of potential sources of information (1.4)

- Applying information in critical thinking and problem solving (3.3)

1B: Students should be able to demonstrate an understanding of the different ways people of diverse racial groups and national origins have transmitted their beliefs and values by:

Students should be able to demonstrate information literacy skills by:

• Explaining the ways that families long ago expressed and transmitted their beliefs through art

• Sharing knowledge and information with others (9.1)

• Comparing dreams and ideals for people from various groups, the problems they encountered, and sources of family strength

• Applying information in critical thinking and problem solving (3.3)

Standard 2: Students should understand the history of their local community and how communities in North America varied long ago.

Students should be able to demonstrate information literacy skills by:

2A: Students should be able to demonstrate an understanding of the history of their local community by:

• Creating a historical narrative about the history of their local community from data gathered through records, documents, etc.

• Developing and using successful strategies for locating information (1.5);
• Producing and communicating information and ideas in appropriate formats (3.4)

• Recording changes in goods and services over time from resources that are available in the local community

• Organizing information for practical applications (3.1)

• Describing local community life long ago, including jobs, schools, communication, religious observances, and recreation

• Producing and communicating information and ideas in appropriate formats (3.4)

• Interpreting population data from historical and current maps, charts, and graphs and then generalizing about changing community

• Integrating new information into one's own knowledge (3.2);
• Applying information in critical thinking and problem solving (3.3)

- Examining local architecture and landscape to compare changes in function and appearance over time

- Applying information in critical thinking and problem solving (3.3)

- Identifying historical figures in the local community and explaining their contributions and significance

- Identifying a variety of potential sources of information (1.4);
- Respecting other's ideas and acknowledging their contributions (9.2)

- Identifying a problem in the community's past, analyzing different perspectives, and evaluating choices and solutions of the people

- Distinguishing among fact, point of view, and opinion (2.2);
- Applying information in critical thinking and problem solving (3.3)

- Comparing and contrasting different ways early Native Americans adapted to their environments and created their community life

- Applying information in critical thinking and problem solving (3.3)

- Drawing upon various sources and describing historical development of a colonial community; creating a historical narrative, mural, etc.

- Developing and using successful strategies for finding information (1.5);
- Producing and communicating information and ideas in appropriate formats (3.4)

- Describing challenges and difficulties encountered by people in pioneer farming communities

- Applying information in critical thinking and problem solving (3.3)

- Drawing upon maps and stories and identifying geographical factors leading to the establishment of mining towns and trading settlements

- Identifying a variety of potential sources of information (1.4);
- Applying information in critical thinking and problem solving (3.3)

- Describing and comparing daily life in ethnically diverse communities long ago (e.g., African-American community in Philadelphia)

- Respecting others' ideas and backgrounds and acknowledging their contributions (9.2)

Standard 3: Students should understand the people, events, problems, and ideas that were significant in creating the history of their state.

3A: Students should be able to demonstrate an understanding of the history of indigenous peoples who first lived in their state or region by:

Students should be able to demonstrate information literacy skills by:

- Drawing upon data in artifacts to hypothesize about the culture of the early Native Americans known to live in their region or state

- Developing and using successful strategies to find information (1.5);
- Applying information in critical thinking and problem solving (3.3)

- Drawing upon legends of the Native Americans in their region/state to describe personal accounts of their history

- Deriving meaning from information presented creatively in a variety of formats (5.2)

- Comparing and contrasting the difference between Native American life today and 100 years ago

- Applying information in critical thinking and problem solving (3.3)

3B: Students should be able to demonstrate an understanding of the history of the first European, African, and/or Asian-Pacific explorers and settlers who came to their state or region by:

Students should be able to demonstrate information literacy skills by:

- Gathering data to analyze geographic, economic, and religious reasons that brought the first settlers to their region or state

- Developing and using successful strategies to find information (1.5);
- Applying information in critical thinking and problem solving (3.3)

- Reconstructing timelines in order of early explorations, settlements, including explorers, and early settlements, and cities

- Organizing information for practical applications (3.1)

- Examining visual data to describe ways in which early settlers adapted to, utilized, and changed the environment

- Producing and communicating information and ideas in appropriate formats (3.4)

- Analyzing some of the interactions that occurred between native peoples and the first explorers/settlers in students' region or state

- Applying information in critical thinking and problem solving (3.3)

- Using a variety of sources to construct historical narrative about daily life in the early settlements in students' region or state

- Seeking information from diverse sources, contexts, disciplines, and cultures (7.1);
- Developing creative products in a variety of formats (5.3)

3C: Students should be able to demonstrate an understanding of the various other groups from regions throughout the world who came into the students' own state or region over the long-ago and recent past by:

Students should be able to demonstrate information literacy skills by:

- Developing a timeline on their region/state and identifying the first inhabitants, successive groups, and significant changes in the region

- Organizing information for practical applications (3.1)

- Using a variety of data, fiction, nonfiction sources, and speakers to identify groups in the region or state and generate ideas why they came

- Seeking information from diverse sources, contexts, disciplines, and cultures (7.1);
- Deriving meaning from information presented creatively in a variety of formats (5.2)

- Examining photos and pictures of ethnic, racial peoples of different socioeconomic status from 100 years ago; hypothesizing about their lives, feelings, and plans and comparing similarities and differences

- Deriving meaning from information presented creatively in a variety of formats (5.2);
- Applying information in critical thinking and problem solving (3.3)

- Examining newspaper and magazine accounts and constructing interview questions for a written or in-person interview with recent immigrants about why they came, their past experiences, and adjustments

- Recognizing need for information (1.1);
- Recognizing accurate information is the basis for intelligent decision making (1.2);
- Formulating questions based on information needs (1.3)

- Drawing upon census data and historical accounts and describing patterns and changes in populations in certain cities, towns, or the students' state

- Describing problems (prejudice and intolerance) and opportunities experienced by groups in their region, in housing, work, etc.

- Drawing on historical narratives and examining sources of strength (family and church, etc.) that groups used to overcome problems

3D: Students should be able to demonstrate an understanding of the interactions among all these groups throughout the history of their state by:

- Listing in chronological order major historical events that are part of the state's history

- Analyzing the significance of major events in the state's history, the impact on people then and now, and the relationship to the history of this nation

- Reading historical narratives to describe how the territory or region attained statehood

- Identifying historical problems and events in the state and analyzing how they were solved and ways they continue to be addressed

- Examining written accounts and identifying and describing regional/state examples of major historical events involving different groups

- Applying information in critical thinking and problem solving (3.3)

- Producing and communicating information and ideas in appropriate formats (3.4)

- Respecting others' ideas and backgrounds and acknowledging their contributions (9.2)

Students should be able to demonstrate information literacy skills by:

- Organizing information for practical applications (3.1)

- Integrating new information into one's own knowledge (3.2);
- Applying information in critical thinking and problem solving (3.3)

- Deriving meaning from information presented creatively in a variety of formats (5.2)

- Integrating new information into one's own knowledge (3.2)

- Selecting information appropriate to the problem or question at hand (2.4);
- Producing and communicating information and ideas in appropriate formats (3.4)

- Investigating the influence of geography on the history of the state or region and identifying issues and approaches to problems like land use

- Applying information in critical thinking and problem solving (3.3)

3E: Students should be able to demonstrate an understanding of the ideas that were significant in the development of the state and that helped to forge its unique identity by:

Students should be able to demonstrate information literacy skills by:

- Drawing upon data to identify symbols, slogans, and mottoes and researching why they represent the state

- Identifying a variety of potential sources of information (1.4);
- Developing and using successful strategies for locating information (1.5)

- Analyzing how the ideas of significant people affected the history of their states

- Applying information in critical thinking and problem solving (3.3)

- Researching in order to explain why important buildings, statues, monuments, and place-names are associated with the state's history

- Identifying a variety of potential sources of information (1.4);
- Determining accuracy, relevancy, and comprehensiveness (2.1)

- Drawing upon a variety of sources to describe the unique historical conditions that influenced formation of the state

- Identifying a variety of potential sources of information (1.4);
- Applying information in critical thinking and problem solving (3.3)

Standard 4: Students should understand how democratic values came to be and how they have been exemplified by people, events, and symbols.

Students should be able to demonstrate information literacy skills by:

4A: Students should be able to demonstrate an understanding of how the U.S. government was formed and of the nation's basic democratic principles set forth in the Declaration of Independence and the Constitution by:

- Explaining the U.S. government was formed by English colonists who fought for independence from England

- Identifying and explaining basic principles that Americans set forth in documents like the Declaration of Independence and the Constitution

- Explaining the importance of basic principles of American democracy that unify us as a nation

- Analyzing how, over the last 200 years, individuals and groups have struggled to achieve liberties and the equality promised by democracy

4B: Students should be able to demonstrate an understanding of ordinary people who have exemplified values and principles of American democracy by:

- Identifying ordinary people who have believed in fundamental democratic values like justice and truth and explaining their significance

- Analyzing, in historical context, the accomplishments of ordinary local people, now and long ago, who helped the common good

- Applying information in critical thinking and problem solving (3.3)

- Respecting the principles of intellectual freedom (8.1);
- Sharing knowledge and information with others (9.1)

- Respecting the principles of intellectual freedom (8.1);
- Sharing knowledge and information with others (9.1)

- Respecting others' ideas and backgrounds and acknowledging their contributions (9.2);
- Applying information in critical thinking and problem solving (3.3)

Students should be able to demonstrate information literacy skills by:

- Respecting others' ideas and backgrounds and acknowledging their contributions (9.2);
- Sharing information with others (9.1)

- Integrating new information into one's own knowledge (3.2);
- Applying information in critical thinking and problem solving (3.3)

4C: Students should be able to demonstrate an understanding of historic figures who have exemplified values and principles of American democracy by:

Students should be able to demonstrate information literacy skills by:

- Identifying historical figures who believed in democratic values and explaining their significance in their historical context and today

- Respecting others' ideas and background and acknowledging their contributions (9.2);
- Applying information in critical thinking and problem solving (3.3)

- Describing how historical figures in the U.S. and other parts of the world have advanced the common good and the character traits that made them successful

- Respecting the principles of intellectual freedom (8.1);
- Applying information in critical thinking and problem solving (3.3)

- Comparing historical biographies and fiction accounts with primary documents to analyze inconsistencies and assess reliability

- Determining accuracy, relevancy, and comprehensiveness (2.1);
- Distinguishing between fact, points of view, and opinions (2.2);
- Identifying inaccurate information (2.3)

4D: Students should be able to demonstrate an understanding of events that celebrate and exemplify fundamental values and principles of American democracy by:

Students should be able to demonstrate information literacy skills by:

- Describing the history of holidays, such as Martin Luther King, Jr. and Presidents' Day, that celebrate the core of democratic values

- Respecting the principles of intellectual freedom (8.1);
- Sharing knowledge and information with others (9.1)

- Describing the history of events, such as the signing of the Mayflower Compact, the Bill of Rights, and the Emancipation Proclamation

- Producing and communicating information and ideas in appropriate formats (3.4)

4E: Students should be able to demonstrate an understanding of national symbols through which American values and principles are expressed by:

- Describing the history of American symbols such as the eagle, the Liberty Bell, and the national flag

- Explaining the connection between important buildings, statues, and monuments and national history (Ellis Island, veteran memorials)

- Analyzing the Pledge of Allegiance, patriotic songs, and poems written long ago to demonstrate an understanding of their significance

- Analyzing songs, symbols, and slogans that demonstrate freedom of expression and the role of protest in democracy

Standard 5: Students should understand the causes and nature of various movements of large groups of people into and within the United States, now and long ago.

5A: Students should be able to demonstrate an understanding of the movements of large groups of people into their own and other states in the United States by:

- Drawing upon data in historical maps, diaries and fiction/nonfiction accounts to chart various movements in the United States

Students should be able to demonstrate information literacy skills by:

- Producing and communicating information and ideas in appropriate formats (3.4)

- Applying information in critical thinking and problem solving (3.3)

- Applying information in critical thinking and problem solving (3.3)

- Respecting the principles of intellectual freedom (8.1);

- Applying information in critical thinking and problem solving (3.3)

Students should be able to demonstrate information literacy skills by:

- Deriving meaning from information presented in a variety of formats (5.2)

- Gathering data to describe the forced relocation of Native Americans and how their lives and rights were affected by European colonization and expansion (i.e., Spanish colonization, Cherokee Trail of Tears, Black Hawk's War)

- Developing and using strategies for locating information (1.5);
- Applying information in critical thinking and problem solving (3.3)

- Drawing upon data from charts, historical maps, and nonfiction and fiction accounts and interviews to describe "through their eyes" the experience of immigrant groups. Include travel experiences, opportunities, and obstacles they faced, etc.

- Developing and using strategies for locating information (1.5);
- Determining accuracy, relevancy, and comprehensiveness (2.1);
- Producing and communicating information and ideas in appropriate formats (3.4)

- Identifying reasons why groups such as freed African Americans, Mexican workers, dust bowl families, etc. migrated to various parts of the country

- Applying information in critical thinking and problem solving (3.3)

- Analyzing the experiences of those who moved from farm to city during periods when the cities grew rapidly in the United States

- Applying information in critical thinking and problem solving (3.3)

Standard 6: Students should understand folklore and other cultural contributions from various regions of the United States and how they help to form a national heritage.

Students should be able to demonstrate information literacy skills by:

6A: Students should be able to demonstrate an understanding of folklore and other cultural contributions from various regions of the United States and how they help to form a national heritage by:

- Describing regional folk heroes, stories, and songs that contributed to development of the cultural history of the United States

- Producing and communicating information and ideas in appropriate formats (3.4)

- Drawing upon stories, legends, ballads, games, and tall tales to describe the environment, lifestyles, and beliefs of people in different regions

- Examining the art, crafts, music, and language of people from a variety of regions long ago and describing their influence on the nation

- Deriving meaning from information presented creatively in a variety of formats (5.2);
- Sharing knowledge and information with others (9.1)

- Deriving meaning from information presented creatively in a variety of formats (5.2);
- Respecting other's ideas and background and acknowledging their contributions (9.2)

Standard 7: Students should understand selected attributes and historical developments of societies in such places as Africa, the Americas, Asia, and Europe.

7A: Students should be able to demonstrate an understanding of the cultures and historical developments of selected societies in such places as Africa, the Americas, Asia, and Europe by:

Students should be able to demonstrate information literacy skills by:

- Investigating the ways historians learn about the past if there are no written records

- Describing the effects geography has on societies, like developments of urban centers, food, trade, shelter, and other aspects

- Comparing and contrasting aspects of family life, structures, and roles in different cultures, in many eras, and with students' own families

- Illustrating or retelling main ideas in folktales, legends, and myths about heroes that tell about the history and traditions of other cultures

- Formulating questions based on information needs (1.3);
- Applying information in critical thinking and problem solving (3.3)

- Selecting information appropriate to the problem or question at hand (2.4)

- Integrating new information into one's own knowledge (3.2)

- Developing creative products in a variety of formats (5.3)

- Describing life in urban areas and communities of various cultures of the world at various times in their history

- Describing significant historical achievements of various cultures of the world

- Analyzing dance, music, and arts of various cultures to draw conclusions about the history and daily life of people in history

- Explaining customs related to important holidays and ceremonies in various countries in the past

7B: Students should be able to demonstrate an understanding of great world movements of people now and long ago by:

- Tracing on maps and explaining migrations of large groups in recent decades

- Drawing upon historical narratives to identify early explorers and describe the knowledge gained from their journeys

- Drawing upon historical narratives to identify European explorers of the 15th and 16th centuries and explaining their reasons for exploring, the knowledge gained from their journeys, and the results of their travel

- Gathering data to explain effects of diffusion of crops and animals between Western and Eastern Hemispheres after Columbus's voyages

- Producing and communicating information and ideas in appropriate formats (3.4)

- Respecting others' ideas and backgrounds and acknowledging their contributions (9.2)

- Deriving meaning from information presented creatively in a variety of formats (5.2)

- Deriving meaning from information presented creatively in a variety of formats (5.2)

Students should be able to demonstrate information literacy skills by:

- Developing and using successful strategies for locating information (1.5);
- Producing and communicating information and ideas in appropriate formats (3.4)

- Deriving meaning from information presented creatively in a variety of formats (5.2)

- Deriving meaning from information presented creatively in a variety of formats (5.2);
- Applying information in critical thinking and problem solving (3.3)

- Developing and using successful strategies for locating information (1.5);
- Applying information in critical thinking and problem solving (3.3)

Standard 8: Students should understand major discoveries in science and technology, some of their social and economic effects, and the major scientists and inventors responsible for them.

8A: Students should be able to demonstrate an understanding of the development of technological innovations, the major scientists and inventors associated with them, and their social and economic effects by:

Students should be able to demonstrate information literacy skills by:

- Comparing and contrasting behaviors of hunters and gatherers with those who cultivated plants and raised domesticated animals

- Applying information in critical thinking and problem solving (3.3)

- Drawing on visual data to illustrate development of the wheel and its early uses in ancient societies

- Deriving meaning from information presented creatively in a variety of formats (5.2)

- Describing the development and influence of basic tools on work and behavior

- Producing and communicating information and ideas in appropriate formats (3.4)

- Identifying and describing technological developments to control fire, water, wind, and utilization of natural resources for human needs

- Applying information in critical thinking and problem solving (3.3)

- Identifying and describing technological inventions and developments that evolved during the 19th century and the effects on workers' lives

- Producing and communicating information and ideas in appropriate formats (3.4)

- Identifying and describing the significant achievements of important scientists and inventors

- Applying information in critical thinking and problem solving (3.3)

8B: Students should be able to demonstrate an understanding of changes in transportation and their effects by:

Students should be able to demonstrate information literacy skills by:

- Creating a timeline showing varieties in forms of transportation and their developments over time

- Organizing information for practical applications (3.1)

- Drawing on photos, illustrations, and non-fiction materials to demonstrate development of marine vessels from ancient times to now

- Deriving meaning from information presented creatively in a variety of formats (5.2);
- Identifying a variety of potential sources of information (1.4)

- Investigating development of extensive road systems and explaining the travel and communication problems over vast expanses and the social and economic effects of these developments

- Developing and using successful strategies for finding information (1.5);
- Applying information in critical thinking and problem solving (3.3)

- Tracing developments in rail transportation in the 19th century and the effects of national systems on the lives of the people

- Organizing information for practical applications (3.1)

- Investigating the design and development of aircraft and the people involved

- Developing and using successful strategies for finding information (1.5)

- Identifying and describing the people who have made significant contributions in the field of transportation

- Respecting others' ideas and backgrounds and acknowledging their contributions (9.2);
- Producing and communicating information and ideas in appropriate formats (3.4)

8C: Students should be able to demonstrate an understanding of changes in communication and their effects by:

- Comparing and contrasting ways people communicate now and long ago, listing in chronological order technology that facilitated developments in communication

- Illustrating the origins and changes in writing methods over time and describing how the changes made communication more effective

- Explaining the significance of the printing press, the computer, and electronic developments in communication and the impact on the spread of ideas

- Comparing and contrasting various systems of long-distance communication and analyzing their effects

- Identifying and describing the people who have made significant contributions in the field of communication

Students should be able to demonstrate information literacy skills by:

- Organizing information for practical applications (3.1)

- Developing creative products in a variety of formats (5.3)

- Applying information in critical thinking and problem solving (3.3)

- Applying information in critical thinking and problem solving (3.3)

- Respecting others' ideas and backgrounds and acknowledging their contributions (9.2);
- Sharing knowledge and information with others (9.1)

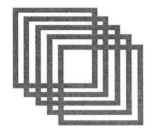

Appendix D: National English Language Arts Standards

The following chart compares the National English Language Arts Standards to the AASL/AECT Information Literacy Standards for Student Learning. Each English language arts standard on the left side of the chart corresponds to the information literacy standard(s) and indicator(s) aligned on the right. There are three types of relationships depicted in the chart: 1) the information literacy standard or indicator *is similar* to the content standard, 2) the information literacy standard or indicator *is necessary to master* the content standard, or 3) the content standard and the information literacy standard(s) or indicator(s) *will be achieved using the same teaching practices*. While the most obvious indicators are listed, there are certainly others that may apply.

This comparison chart may be used in conjunction with the Checklist of Information Literacy Goals, Objectives, and Strategies found in chapter 8. Together the chart and the checklist become valuable tools for planning units and lessons that integrate information literacy skills into the subject-area curriculum.

Standards for the English Language Arts, by the International Reading Association and the National Council of Teachers of English, Copyright 1996 by the International Reading Association and the National Council of Teachers of English. Reprinted with permission.

The AASL/AECT Information Literacy Standards are from *Information Power: Building Partnerships for Learning* by American Association of School Libraries and Association for Educational Communications and Technology. Copyright © 1998 American Library Association and Association for Educational Communications and Technology. Reprinted by permission of the American Library Association.

LANGUAGE ARTS

NCTE ENGLISH LANGUAGE ARTS STANDARDS	AASL/AECT INFORMATION LITERACY STANDARDS

Standard 1

Students should read a wide range of print and nonprint texts to:

Information-literate students should:

- Build an understanding of texts, of themselves, and of the cultures of the United States and the world

- Recognize a need for information (1.1);
- Recognize that accurate and comprehensive information is the basis for intelligent decision making (1.2)

- Acquire new information

- Seek information from diverse sources, contexts, disciplines, and cultures (7.1)

- Respond to the needs and demands of society and the workplace and for personal fulfillment

- Seek information related to various dimensions of personal well-being (4.1)

- Gain exposure to fiction and nonfiction, classic and contemporary works

- Seek information from diverse sources, contexts, disciplines, and cultures (7.1)

Standard 2

Students should read a wide range of literature from many periods in many genres to:

Information-literate students should:

- Build an understanding of the many dimensions (philosophical and ethical) of the human experience

- Derive meaning from information presented creatively in a variety of formats (5.2);
- Seek information from diverse sources, contexts, disciplines, and cultures (7.1)

Standard 3

Students should apply a wide range of strategies to comprehend, interpret, evaluate, and appreciate texts by drawing on:

Information-literate students should:

- Their past experiences and their interactions with other readers and writers

- Integrate new information into one's own knowledge (3.2)

- Their knowledge of word meaning and of other texts, their word identification strategies, and their understanding of textual features

- Apply information in critical thinking and problem solving (3.3)

Standard 4

Students should:

Information-literate students should:

- Adjust their use of spoken, written, and visual language to communicate effectively with a variety of audiences and for different purposes

- Produce and communicate information and ideas in appropriate formats (3.4)

Standard 5

Students should:

Information-literate students should:

- Employ a wide range of strategies as they write

- Organize information for practical applications (3.1)

- Use different writing process elements appropriately to communicate with different audiences for a variety of purposes

- Produce and communicate information and ideas in appropriate formats (3.4);
- Develop creative products in a variety of formats (5.3)

Standard 6

Students should apply knowledge of:

Information-literate students should:

- Language structure, language conventions, and media techniques

- Integrate new information into one's own knowledge (3.2)

- Figurative language and genre to create, critique, and discuss print and nonprint texts

- Derive meaning from information presented creatively in a variety of formats (5.2);
- Apply information in critical thinking and problem solving (3.3)

Standard 7

Students should:

- Conduct research on issues and interests by generating ideas and questions and by posing problems

- Evaluate and synthesize data from a variety of sources to communicate their discoveries in ways that suit their purpose and audience

Information-literate students should:

- Formulate questions based on information needs (1.3);
- Identify a variety of sources of information (1.4);
- Develop and use successful strategies for locating information (1.5)

- Determine accuracy, relevance, and comprehensiveness (2.1);
- Organize information for practical applications (3.1);
- Produce and communicate information and ideas in a variety of formats (3.4)

Standard 8

Students should:

- Use a variety of technological and informational sources to gather and synthesize information and to create and communicate knowledge

Information-literate students should:

- Seek information from diverse sources, contexts, disciplines, and cultures (7.1);
- Share knowledge and information with others (9.1);
- Use information technology responsibly (8.3)

Standard 9

Students should develop an understanding of and respect for:

- Diversity in language use, patterns, and dialects across cultures, ethnic groups, geographic regions, and social roles

Information-literate students should:

- Derive meaning from information presented creatively in a variety of formats (5.2);
- Respect others' ideas and backgrounds and acknowledge their contributions (9.2)

Standard 10

Students whose first language is not English should make use of their first language to:

- Develop competency in the English language arts and develop an understanding of content across the curriculum

Information-literate students should:

- Integrate new information into one's own knowledge (3.2);
- Devise strategies for revising, improving, and updating self-generated knowledge (6.2)

Standard 11

Students should participate as:

- Knowledgable, reflective, creative, and critical members of a variety of literacy communities

Information-literate students should:

- Collaborate with others, both in person and through technologies, to design, develop, and evaluate information products and solutions (9.4)

Standard 12

Students should use:

- Spoken, written, and visual language to accomplish their own purposes

Information-literate students should:

- Design, develop, and evaluate information products and solutions related to personal interests (4.2)

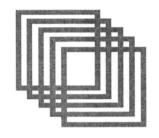

Appendix E: National Fine Arts Standards

The following chart compares the National Fine Arts Standards to the AASL/AECT Information Literacy Standards for Student Learning. Each fine arts standard on the left side of the chart corresponds to the information literacy standard(s) and indicator(s) aligned on the right. There are three types of relationships depicted in the chart: 1) the information literacy standard or indicator *is similar* to the content standard, 2) the information literacy standard or indicator *is necessary to master* the content standard, or 3) the content standard and the information literacy standard(s) or indicator(s) *will be achieved using the same teaching practices*. While the most obvious indicators are listed, there are certainly others that may apply.

The National Fine Arts Standards are reprinted with permission from *National Standards for Arts Education*. Copyright 1994 by the National Consortium for Arts Education.

The visual arts standards are used with permission from the National Visual Arts Standards (Reston, VA: National Art Education Association, 1994).

The music standards are excerpted from *National Standards for Arts Education*, published by Music Educators National Conference (MENC). Copyright © 1994 by MENC. Reproduced with permission. The complete National Arts Standards and additional materials relating to the Standards are available from MENC—The National Association for Music Education, 1806 Robert Fulton Drive, Reston, VA 20191 (telephone 800-336-3768).

The theater standards are used with permission from the American Alliance for Theatre and Education.

The AASL/AECT Information Literacy Standards are from *Information Power: Building Partnerships for Learning* by American Association of School Libraries and Association for Educational Communications and Technology. Copyright © 1998 American Library Association and Association for Educational Communications and Technology. Reprinted by permission of the American Library Association.

ART CONNECTIONS STANDARDS

FINE ARTS STANDARDS	AASL/AECT INFORMATION LITERACY STANDARDS
Standard 1: Understands connections among the various forms and other disciplines	**An information-literate student:**
• Knows how visual, aural, oral, and kinetic elements are used in the various art forms	• Derives meaning from information presented in a variety of formats (5.2)
• Knows how ideas are expressed in the various art forms	• Produces and communicates information and ideas in appropriate formats (3.4); • Develops creative products in a variety of formats (5.3)
• Knows the similarities and differences in the meanings of common terms used in the various art forms	• Applies information in critical thinking and problem solving (3.3)
• Knows ways in which the principles and subject matter of other disciplines taught in the school are interrelated with those of the arts (e.g., pattern in the arts and in science)	• Appreciates literature and other creative expressions of information (5.0); • Integrates new information into one's own knowledge (3.2)

DANCE STANDARDS

FINE ARTS STANDARDS	AASL/AECT INFORMATION LITERACY STANDARDS
Dance Standard 1: Identifies and demonstrates movement elements and skills in performing dance	**An information-literate student:**
• Knows basic nonlocomotor/axial movements	• Integrates new information into one's own knowledge (3.2); • Uses information effectively and creatively (3.0)

- Knows basic locomotor movements and different directions in which they can be performed

- Creates shapes at low, middle, and high levels (different heights from the floor)

- Defines and maintains personal space

- Uses movement in straight and curved pathways

- Moves to a rhythmic accompaniment and responds to changes in tempo

- Uses kinesthetic awareness, concentration, and focus in performing movement skills

- Knows basic actions and movement elements and how they communicate ideas

Dance Standard 2: Understands choreographic principles, processes, and structures

- Creates a sequence with a beginning, middle, and ending

- Improvises, creates, and performs dances based on personal ideas and concepts from other sources

- Knows how improvisation is used to discover and invent movement and to solve movement problems

- Integrates new information into one's own knowledge (3.2);
- Uses information effectively and creatively (3.0)

- Produces and communicates information and ideas in appropriate formats (3.4)

- Selects information appropriate to the problem or question at hand (2.4)

- Strives for excellence in information seeking and knowledge generation (6.0)

- Produces and communicates information and ideas in appropriate formats (3.4)

An information-literate student:

- Organizes information for practical applications (3.1)

- Designs and develops products and solutions related to personal interests (4.2);
- Pursues information related to personal interests (4.0)

- Applies information in critical thinking and problem solving (3.3)

- Creates a dance phrase, repeats it, and varies it

- Develops creative products in a variety of formats (5.3);
- Applies information in critical thinking and problem solving (3.3)

- Uses partner skills such as copying, leading and following, and mirroring

- Participates effectively in groups to generate information (9.0)

Dance Standard 3: Understands dance as a way to create and communicate meaning

An information-literate student:

- Knows how dance is different from other forms of human movement

- Selects information appropriate to the problem or question at hand (2.4);
- Integrates new information into one's own knowledge (3.2)

- Knows how a dance may elicit various interpretations and reactions that differ from the meaning intended by the dancer

- Derives meaning from information presented creatively in a variety of formats (5.2);
- Develops creative products in a variety of formats (5.3)

Dance Standard 4: Applies critical- and creative-thinking skills in dance

An information-literate student:

- Knows how a variety of solutions can be used to solve a given movement problem

- Identifies a variety of potential sources of information (1.4);
- Selects information appropriate to the problem or question at hand (2.4);
- Applies information in critical thinking and problem solving (3.3)

- Knows technical and artistic components of various forms of dance

- Recognizes that accurate and comprehensive information is the basis for intelligent decision making (1.2)

Dance Standard 5: Understands dance in various cultures and historical periods

An information-literate student:

- Knows folk dances from various cultures

- Seeks information from diverse sources, contexts, disciplines, and cultures (7.1)

- Knows the cultural and/or historical context of various dances

- Respects others' ideas and backgrounds and acknowledges their contributions (9.2)

Dance Standard 6: Understands connections between dance and healthful living

An information-literate student:

- Knows how healthy practices enhance the ability to dance

- Pursues information related to personal interests (4.0)

MUSIC STANDARDS

FINE ARTS STANDARDS	AASL/AECT INFORMATION LITERACY STANDARDS

Music Standard 1: Sings, alone and with others, a varied repertoire of music

An information-literate student:

- Sings ostinatos, partner songs, and rounds

- Appreciates literature and other creative expressions of information (5.0)

- Sings on pitch and in rhythm, with appropriate timbre, diction, and posture, and maintains a steady tempo

- Produces and communicates information and ideas in appropriate formats (3.4)

- Sings expressively, with appropriate dynamics, phrasing, and interpretation

- Develops creative products in a variety of formats (5.3)

- Blends vocal timbres, matches dynamic levels, and responds to the cues of a conductor when singing as part of a group

- Participates effectively in groups to pursue and generate information (9.0)

- Knows songs representing genres and styles from diverse cultures

- Seeks information from diverse sources, contexts, disciplines, and cultures (7.1);

- Respects others' ideas and backgrounds and acknowledges their contributions (9.2)

Music Standard 2: Performs on instruments, alone and with others, a varied repertoire of music

An information-literate student:

- Echoes short rhythms and melodic patterns

- Produces and communicates information and ideas in appropriate formats (3.4)

- Performs on pitch, in rhythm, with appropriate dynamics and timbre, and maintains a steady tempo

- Develops creative products in a variety of formats (5.3)

- Performs simple rhythmic, melodic, and chordal patterns accurately and independently on classroom instruments

- Uses information technology responsibly (8.3)

- Knows a varied repertoire of music representing diverse genres and styles

- Integrates new information into one's own knowledge (3.2);

- Seeks information from diverse sources, contexts, disciplines, and cultures (7.1)

- Performs in groups

- Participates effectively in groups to pursue and generate information (9.0)

- Performs independent instrumental parts while others sing or play contrasting parts

- Uses information technology responsibly (8.3);

- Collaborates with others to design, develop, and evaluate information products and solutions (9.4)

Music Standard 3: Improvises melodies, variations, and accompaniments

An information-literate student:

- Improvises "answers" in the same style to given rhythmic and melodic phrases

- Selects information appropriate to the problem or question at hand (2.4);
- Produces and communicates information and ideas in appropriate formats (3.4)

- Improvises simple rhythmic and melodic ostinato accompaniments

- Develops creative products in a variety of formats (5.3);
- Collaborates with others to design, develop, and evaluate information products and solutions (9.4)

- Improvises simple rhythmic variations and simple melodic embellishments on familiar melodies

- Applies information in critical thinking and problem solving (3.3)

- Improvises short songs and instrumental pieces using a variety of sound sources, including traditional sounds, nontraditional sounds, body sounds, and sounds produced by electronic means

- Develops creative products in a variety of formats (5.3);
- Uses information technology responsibly (8.3)

Music Standard 4: Composes and arranges music within specified guidelines

An information-literate student:

- Uses a variety of sound sources when composing

- Identifies a variety of potential sources of information (1.4);
- Develops creative products in a variety of formats (5.3);
- Uses information technology responsibly (8.3)

- Creates and arranges music to accompany readings or dramatizations

- Produces and communicates information and ideas in appropriate formats (3.4)

- Creates and arranges short songs and instrumental pieces within specified guidelines

- Recognizes the need for information (1.1);
- Formulates questions based on information needs (1.3);
- Selects information appropriate to the problem or question at hand (2.4);
- Applies information in critical thinking and problem solving (3.3)

Music Standard 5: Reads and notates music

An information-literate student:

- Knows standard symbols used to notate meter, rhythm, pitch, and dynamics in simple patterns

- Integrates new information into one's own knowledge (3.2);
- Organizes information for practical applications (3.1)

- Uses a system to read simple pitch notation in the treble clef in major keys

- Selects information appropriate to the problem or question at hand (2.4);
- Applies information in critical thinking and problem solving (3.3)

- Reads whole, half, dotted half, quarter, and eighth notes and rests in 2/4, 3/4, and 4/4 meter signatures

- Derives meaning from information presented creatively in a variety of formats (5.2)

- Knows symbols and traditional terms referring to dynamics, tempo, and articulation

- Derives meaning from information presented creatively in a variety of formats (5.2);
- Integrates new information into one's own knowledge (3.2)

Music Standard 6: Knows and applies appropriate criteria in music and music performances

An information-literate student:

- Knows personal preferences for specific musical works and styles

- Seeks information related to personal interests (4.0)

- Identifies simple music forms when presented aurally

- Derives meaning from information presented creatively in a variety of formats (5.2)

- Responds through purposeful movement to selected prominent music characteristics or to specific music events

- Selects information appropriate to the problem or question at hand (2.4)

- Knows music of various styles representing diverse cultures

- Derives meaning from information presented creatively in a variety of formats (5.2);
- Seeks information from diverse sources, contexts, disciplines, and cultures (7.1)

- Knows appropriate terminology used to explain music, music notation, music instruments and voices, and music performances

- Selects information appropriate to the problem or question at hand (2.4)

- Identifies the sounds of a variety of instruments and voices

- Derives meaning from information presented creatively in a variety of formats (5.2)

Music Standard 7: Understands the relationship between music and history and culture

An information-literate student:

- Knows characteristics that make certain music suitable for specific uses

- Evaluates information critically and competently (2.0);
- Uses information accurately and creatively (3.0)

- Knows appropriate audience behavior for the context and style of music performed

- Appreciates creative expressions of information (5.0);
- Respects the principle of equitable access to information (7.2)

- Identifies music from various historical periods and cultures

- Seeks information from diverse sources, contexts, disciplines, and cultures (7.1);
- Integrates new information into one's own knowledge (3.2)

- Knows how basic elements of music are used in music from various cultures of the world

- Applies information in critical thinking and problem solving (3.3)

- Understands the roles of musicians in various music settings and cultures

- Respects others' ideas and backgrounds and acknowledges their contributions (9.2)

THEATER STANDARDS

FINE ARTS STANDARDS	AASL/AECT INFORMATION LITERACY STANDARDS

Theater Standard 1: Demonstrates competence in writing scripts

An information-literate student:

- Selects interrelated characters, environments, and situations for simple dramatizations

- Identifies a variety of potential sources of information (1.4);
- Selects appropriate information (2.4)

- Improvises dialogue to tell stories

- Organizes information for practical applications (3.1)

- Writes or records dialogue

- Produces and communicates information and ideas in appropriate formats (3.4)

- Plans and records improvisations based on personal experience and heritage, imagination, literature, and history

- Designs, develops, and evaluates information products related to personal interests (4.2)

Theater Standard 2: Uses acting skills

An information-literate student:

- Knows characters in dramatizations, their relationships, and their environments

- Seeks information from diverse sources, contexts, disciplines, and cultures (7.1)

- Uses variations of locomotor and nonlocomotor movement and vocal pitch, tempo, and tone for different characters

- Applies information in critical thinking and problem solving (3.3);
- Develops creative products in a variety of formats (5.3)

- Assumes roles that exhibit concentration and contribute to the action of dramatizations based on personal experience and heritage, imagination, literature, and history

- Identifies a variety of potential sources of information (1.4);
- Selects appropriate information (2.4);
- Strives for excellence in information seeking and knowledge generation (6.0)

- Knows how to interact in improvisations

- Produces and communicates information and ideas in appropriate formats (3.4)

Theater Standard 3: Designs and produces informal and formal productions

An information-literate student:

- Knows how visual elements and aural aspects are used to communicate locale and mood

- Selects appropriate information (2.4);
- Produces and communicates information and ideas in appropriate formats (3.4)

- Selects and organizes available materials that suggest scenery, properties, lighting, sound, costumes, and makeup

- Identifies a variety of potential sources of information (1.4);
- Selects appropriate information (2.4);
- Organizes information for practical applications (3.1)

- Visualizes and arranges environments for classroom dramatizations

- Develops creative products in a variety of formats (5.3)

Theater Standard 4: Directs scenes and productions

An information-literate student:

- Knows various ways of staging classroom dramatizations
- Plans and prepares improvisations

- Uses information effectively and creatively (3.0)

Theater Standard 5: Understands how informal and formal theater, film, television, and electronic media production create and communicate meaning

An information-literate student:

- Understands the visual, aural, oral, and kinetic elements of dramatic performances

- Derives meaning from information presented in a variety of formats (5.2)

- Understands how the wants and needs of characters are similar to and different from one's own wants and needs

- Evaluates information critically and competently (2.0)

- Provides rationales for personal preferences about the whole as well as the parts of dramatic performance

- Applies information in critical thinking and problem solving (3.3)

- Knows how alternative ideas can be used to enhance character roles, environments, and situations

- Respects principles of intellectual freedom (8.1);
- Organizes information for practical applications (3.1)

- Knows appropriate terminology used in analyzing dramatizations

- Integrates new information into one's own knowledge (3.2)

- Identifies people, events, time, and place in classroom dramatizations

- Derives meaning from information presented creatively in a variety of formats (5.2)

Theater Standard 6: Understands the context in which theater, film, television, and electronic media are performed today as well as in the past

An information-literate student:

- Identifies and compares similar characters and situations in stories/dramas from and about various cultures

- Respects others' ideas and backgrounds and acknowledges their contributions (9.2);
- Organizes information for practical applications (3.1);
- Applies information in critical thinking and problem solving (3.3)

- Understands the various settings and reasons for creating dramas and attending theater, film, television, and electronic media productions

- Applies information in critical thinking and problem solving (3.3)

- Knows ways in which theater reflects life

- Integrates new information into one's own knowledge (3.2)

VISUAL ARTS STANDARDS

FINE ARTS STANDARDS	AASL/AECT INFORMATION LITERACY STANDARDS
Visual Arts Content Standard 1: Understanding and applying media, techniques, and processes	**An information-literate student:**
• Achievement Standard: Know the differences between materials, techniques, and processes	• Selects appropriate information (2.4)
• Describe how different materials, techniques, and processes cause different responses	• Uses information effectively and creatively (3.0)
• Use art materials and tools in a safe and responsible manner	• Organizes information for practical applications (3.1)
Visual Arts Content Standard 2: Using knowledge of structures and functions	**An information-literate student:**
• Achievement Standard: Know the differences among visual characteristics and purposes of art in order to convey ideas	• Evaluates information critically and competently (2.0)
• Describe how different expressive features and organizational principles cause different responses	• Derives meaning from information presented creatively in a variety of formats (5.2); • Uses information effectively and creatively (3.0)
• Use visual structures and functions of art to communicate ideas	• Develops creative products in a variety of formats (5.3)

Visual Arts Content Standard 3: Choosing and evaluating a range of subject matter, symbols, and ideas

An information-literate student:

- Achievement Standard: Explore and understand prospective content for works of art

- Identifies a variety of potential sources of information (1.4);
- Selects appropriate information (2.4)

- Select and use subject matter, symbols, and ideas to communicate meaning

- Uses information effectively and creatively (3.0)

Visual Arts Content Standard 4: Understanding the visual arts in relation to history and cultures

An information-literate student:

- Achievement Standard: Know that the visual arts have both a history and specific relationships to various cultures

- Respects others' ideas and backgrounds and acknowledges their contributions (9.2)

- Identify specific works of art as belonging to particular cultures, times, and places

- Evaluates information critically and competently (2.0);
- Applies information in critical thinking and problem solving (3.3)

- Demonstrate how history, culture, and the visual arts can influence each other in making and studying works of art

- Derives meaning from information presented creatively in a variety of formats (5.2)

Visual Arts Content Standard 5: Reflecting upon and assessing the characteristics and merits of their work and the work of others

An information-literate student:

- Achievement Standard: Understand various purposes for creating works of visual art

- Pursues information related to personal interests (4.0)

- Describe how people's experiences influence the development of specific artworks

- Derives meaning from information presented creatively in a variety of formats (5.2)

- Understand there are different responses to specific artworks

- Evaluates information critically and competently (2.0)

Visual Arts Content Standard 6: Making connections between visual arts and other disciplines

An information-literate student:

- Achievement Standard: Understand and use similarities and differences between characteristics of the visual arts and other arts disciplines

- Derives meaning from information presented creatively in a variety of formats (5.2)

- Identify connections between the visual arts and other disciplines in the curriculum

- Evaluates information critically and competently (2.0)

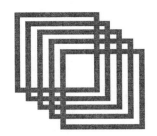

Appendix
F

As noted in chapter 5, library media specialists are natural leaders in the information literacy movement. The following transparency masters are designed to assist library media specialists in introducing and explaining the concepts and components of a school-wide information literacy program.

The transparencies may be used as is, enhanced with graphics, or personalized with school logos. The transparencies, and a PowerPoint version, are also included on the disk that came with this book.

INFORMATION LITERACY

IN-SERVICE

WHAT IS

INFORMATION LITERACY?

Information Literacy
is the ability to
- **access**
- **evaluate**

and

- **use**

information from
a variety of sources
for both

- **academic**

and

- **personal reasons**

and to effectively

- **communicate**

this knowledge to others.

From *Fostering Information Literacy: Connecting National Standards, Goals 2000, and the SCANS Report.* © 2000 Libraries Unlimited. (800) 237-6124.

What is access?

Defining a need

Asking a question

Locating information resources

What is evaluation?

Selecting and judging information

Evaluating process and product of information gathering

What is use?

Organizing information

Applying information in critical thinking and problem solving

Communicating and using information effectively

CHARACTERISTICS OF AN INFORMATION-LITERATE PERSON

1. *Accesses information* efficiently and effectively

2. *Evaluates information* critically and competently

3. *Uses information* effectively and creatively

From *AASL/AECT Information Literacy Standards for Student Learning.*

4. *Pursues information*
related to personal interests

5. *Appreciates and*
enjoys literature
and other creative expressions of information

6. *Strives for excellence*
in information seeking and knowledge generation

From *AASL/AECT Information Literacy Standards for Student Learning*.

7. *Recognizes the importance of information* in a democratic society

8. *Practices ethical behavior* in regard to information and information technology

9. *Participates effectively in groups* to pursue and generate information

From *AASL/AECT Information Literacy Standards for Student Learning.*

An information-literate person has "learned to learn."

An information-literate person follows steps or a path when learning new information.

STEPS IN THE LEARNING (RESEARCH) PROCESS

- **Define a need or ask a question**

- **Locate and access information resources**

- **Select and evaluate information**

- **Organize information**

- **Communicate and use information**

- **Evaluate the process and product of information gathering**

From *Fostering Information Literacy: Connecting National Standards, Goals 2000, and the SCANS Report.* © 2000 Libraries Unlimited. (800) 237-6124.

WHY IS

INFORMATION

LITERACY

IMPORTANT

AND NECESSARY?

GOALS 2000

"By the year 2000, every adult will be literate and will possess the knowledge and skills necessary to compete in a global economy and exercise the rights and responsibilities of citizenship."

SCANS REPORT

Competencies necessary for future workers include *Acquiring*, *Evaluating*, *Interpreting*, and *Communicating* knowledge.

A NATION PREPARED

"People . . . will not come to the workplace knowing all they have to know, but knowing how to figure out what they need to know, where to get it, and how to make meaning out of it."

REQUIREMENTS OF AN INFORMATION LITERACY PROGRAM

Student-centered curriculum

Problem-solving activities

Resource-based curriculum

Critical- and creative-thinking skills instruction

Multiple technology access

Hands-on learning experiences

Integrated curriculum units

Teacher/library media specialist collaboration

HOW CAN WE ENSURE OUR STUDENTS ARE

INFORMATION LITERATE?

HOW CAN WE TEACH THEM TO BE

EFFECTIVE USERS OF KNOWLEDGE AND IDEAS?

Plan and Teach

INTEGRATED UNITS OF STUDY

Integrate
Information Literacy
Skills and Objectives

into

Subject-Area Curriculum Units

THINGS TO CONSIDER

Multiple Intelligences

Linguistic

Logical-Mathematical

Spatial

Musical

Bodily-Kinesthetic

Interpersonal

Intrapersonal

Naturalistic

THINGS TO CONSIDER

Different Learning Styles

Auditory linguistic

Visual linguistic

Auditory numerical

Visual numerical

Audiovisual-kinesthetic combination

Individual learner

Group learner

Oral expressive

Written expressive

THINGS TO CONSIDER

Critical-Thinking Skills (Bloom's Taxonomy)

Knowledge

Comprehension

Application

Analysis

Synthesis

Evaluation

From *Fostering Information Literacy: Connecting National Standards, Goals 2000, and the SCANS Report.* © 2000 Libraries Unlimited. (800) 237-6124.

THINGS TO CONSIDER

Different Levels of
Information Literacy Development

Beginner

Intermediate

Advanced

Need Specifics?

Refer to your

Checklist
of
Information Literacy
Skills

Need more information?

See
your friendly

Library Media
Specialist!

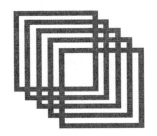

Appendix
G

Appendix G outlines the major concepts of information literacy and lists the components necessary to implement a school-wide program. This handout is designed to be distributed during an information literacy in-service or presentation. It may be used as is, enhanced with graphics, or personalized with school logos. An electronic version of the handout is included on the disk that came with this book.

INFORMATION LITERACY

DEFINITION

Information Literacy is the ability to
access
evaluate
and
use
information from a *variety of sources* for
both
academic
and
personal reasons
and to effectively
communicate
this knowledge to others.

REQUIREMENTS OF AN INFORMATION LITERACY PROGRAM

- Student-centered curriculum
- Problem-solving activities
- Resource-based curriculum
- Critical- and creative-thinking skills instruction
- Multiple technology access
- Hands-on learning experiences
- Integrated curriculum units
- Teacher/library media specialist collaboration

THE LEARNING (RESEARCH) PROCESS

1. Appreciating/Enjoying Information
   …viewing, listening, reading
2. Wondering/Asking Questions
   …defining the need for information
3. Background Building
   …getting an overview
4. Seeking Information
   …locating and accessing resources
5. Understanding/Appraising Information
   …choosing, selecting, evaluating
6. Organizing/Using Information
   …connecting useful information
7. Communicating Information
   …repackaging and sharing
8. Evaluating the Process and the Product
   …reflecting on the search and the project
9. Formulating New Questions
   …continuing the research cycle

AN

INFORMATION-LITERATE

PERSON

HAS

"LEARNED TO LEARN"

From *Fostering Information Literacy: Connecting National Standards, Goals 2000, and the SCANS Report.* © 2000 Libraries Unlimited. (800) 237-6124.

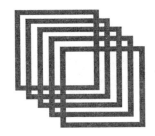

Index